Become Your Own Bank By Learning To Make Money Online Today!

Anthony Bissong

ISBN:1463749481
ISBN-13:978-1463749484

DEDICATION

This book is dedicated to my dad a remarkable individual, who accomplished unbelievable things, during his amazing life.
Anthony O Bissong.

CONTENTS

Acknowledgments   i

1   Introduction   1

2   Goals Make You Rich   Pg 11

3   Dig For Gold   Pg 22

4   Become Famous Through Your Online Business   Pg 48

5   How To Start Printing Money By Converting Traffic   Pg 78

6   Slick Technology Behind Your Online Riches   Pg 88

7   Begin To Understand How To Protect Your Wealth   Pg 106

8   Conclusion   Pg 113

Appendix   Pg 115

ACKNOWLEDGMENTS

A book of this nature owes a debt of gratitude to a number of people that have made it possible. First among those is to my wife, for her love, the emotional support and the editorial overview provided in completion of the book. To my children for their love and innocent view of the world, which brings me so much joy. Finally to my dear mother, for her unyielding love and support

1 INTRODUCTION

Congratulation on becoming rich. "What!" May quite likely be your response with a sense of disbelief. Well I believe in you, because you are a seeker of knowledge. I also know the book to be full of ideas regarding making money online, and you only need one to become rich. So I am brave enough to say the chances of you achieving this are quite high.

Interestingly, we are at a juncture when some may feel it is not the right time to start a business. This is partly, to do with conventional wisdoms and innate fear. If only conventional wisdom made us money, we will all be better for it.

Yet nothing could be further from the truth. History is replete with businesses starting during so called downturns and going on to be tremendously successful. There is some logic to this.

Imagine been able to run a business through what most see as a difficult patch, when the good times come, which there invariably do, you will be in good stead to cleanup on the opportunities on offer, due to the experience garnered from the prior down patch.

It is sort of a Darwinian process where your business is made stronger by surviving what some deem a difficult time. Hence, starting a business now more so than ever, may be a good time to cut your teeth as an entrepreneur.

Ever wondered why some still prosper under any condition. They do so, because the glass for them is never half empty. It is only half full at the least. Never half empty. These clear sighted see opportunities where others choose to indulge in despair.

As we speak sharp minded individuals are seizing the moment by taking advantage of once in a life time opportunities, which you too can also take advantage of.

Some of these opportunities naturally ranges from the fact that certain inefficient businesses that were able to survive during the period of largesse, may not be readily amenable to present conditions, thus creating an opportunity for your business.

Also the change in conditions, brings new opportunities , by way of people looking for new ways of doing things, which in turn may present opportunities, specifically for online businesses. Who knows you could be the next Microsoft or Apple, faced with similar times as the present.

But what should not be forgotten, in all this, is that people always need things regardless of the prevailing conditions. And you can provide for them with what they want. I will show you in this book, how to find those people that will make you rich.

However, in order to capitalize on this moment and any other time for that matter, having the right mindset is an absolute must. Most people, looking to start a business have very modest goals. Like the intention of simply using the business in this case online home business, as a mechanism for covering basic expenses.

To this, I will say there almost is no point starting a business based on such modest goal. The work involved starting and running a successful business simply does not justify such low ambition.

Rather you should be ambitious enough to stretch yourself, and make the journey of running your online business meaningful. This book is all about setting big goals and putting the effort to achieve them. I make no apologies for this.

Another mistake most make, is wanting instant gratification from running a multimillion dollar online business within a year of starting. What is even worse, is the refusal to put in some effort.

This invariably leads to unnecessary disappointments, as they end up overestimating what can be achieved within a short period as consequence underestimating what can be achieve over the long term. The key is to maintain a healthy level of balance between short term objectives and long term goals.

On observation, some of the issues encountered around the levels of ambition required to drive your business, could be put down to misplaced beliefs about being rich. Add to that, a lack of understanding of what's required in getting rich. In this case, a lack of understanding of how to get rich from your online business.

Regarding the issue of misplaced belief, what is mostly not understood, is that there are certain insecurities every person need to address. The essence of a balanced life relies on this to be achieved. But in order to achieve this you need to satisfy your basic needs of financial security. Without addressing this, you are probably not likely to address other areas of your life. So do not feel guilty thinking big and having a vision of a complete life. Complementing this with setting the right goals to achieve financial security through your online business.

Beyond defining the right goals or visions for your online business, this book looks to provide a stepped approach for starting and running a successful online business. However, following the steps is not enough, you will need to have a relentless energy that is focused on wanting to succeed with your online business. I know you are a winner, and I am confident you will succeed and enjoy life to its fullest. I know this because all you are after is the knowledge to make money. Your wisdom already sees passion and energy as implicit to this goal.

Unlike majority who may start with the intention of trying something, which by the way I truly believe is one of the biggest reason of failure. You on the other hand are not looking to try, instead you are resolved to becoming rich online. And why not if anybody is to be rich out of your online business, it might as well be you.

My advice to the majority looking to "try" running an online business, has always been the same. "Best to wait until you are sure you are ready to run an online business. There is no room to be lukewarm with your online business or any other business." You have to resolve yourself to a point of dare I say obsession over your online business.

It is also very important to appreciate that, to become wealthy through your online business, does not depend on you having money, being at the right place at the right time or even the state of the economy. That is not what is required to be a success online entrepreneur.

The most important determinant for starting and continuously printing money through your online business, is for you to think and act correctly. You would have seen I said think and act correctly here, as thinking without acting on your thoughts is foolhardy. All things said, it is of utmost importance that you develop your mind and continuously do so, in order to get sound ideas to expand the wealth generation capability of your online business.

An open mind is required to start the process of thinking correctly. We begin by asking a fundamental question, just like the ever inquisitive Socrates, whose relentless quest for knowledge, led to the creation of wealth in our times, beyond what was deemed possible, even by king Midas.

The question simply put, is why are some more successful in anything they set their mind on, while others are less successful? Why do some have all the wealth imaginable, while others scrape for a living. The real significant reason for this, can be seen throughout the ages. Bold enlightened sage have come to understand it as the infinite "life principle" that moves the universe and of the untold opportunities and possibilities it opens up to them.

The principle is used successfully in present times, by revered businessmen, admirable scientist, top innovators and cerebral bankers. The same principle can be used online with assured wealth and status as a result.

The following paragraphs outline the elements behind this principle. However deeper revelations, are uncovered within subsequent chapters of the book. With the aim of guiding you to becoming a master within the exciting world of cyber space.

Beyond our internal reality exist an external independent reality. This reality is full of abundance of limitless wealth. It is able to supply all we ask for with no exception. Firstly you have to truly believe that you are not limited by your circumstance, or what appears to be limited supply in your internal reality. Accept and believe that there is an abundant supply of everything and anything you may need, and it is all there for the taking if you would but ask for it.

I know this is challenging for some, right from birth you may have been condition to believe in limitation. But you have to start from this premise to guide your overall approach for starting and running a successful online business. When you think of it, it does not require any more from you at this point, other than to belief you can achieve an aspiration of starting and running a successful online business that is not limited by your beliefs.

Next, you have to think and have a vision of what it is you want. What exactly do you want to achieve in life. Really make this vision as clear as you can in your mind, fix your whole concentration on this one vision and truly believe you are living the vision in question. You will be carrying out a goal setting exercise in the next chapter which is underpinned by having a vision of where you would like to be as the consequence of running a successful online business.

Thirdly you have to make a conscious effort of submitting this vision to the super consciousness or God if you are of a religious disposition. The only way to submit your vision to the super consciousness and get the super consciousness to provide what you ask for, is to have total clarity and unshakable believe, that what you have asked for will come to fruition in your life. As an example, if you would like to own a beautiful home, you will need to be specific. Provide as much details as you can, and submit it to the super consciousness through your thoughts.

Some of the details, may be your love of exotic places, preferable one with crisp white sand beach next to a clear blue sea. If so you imagine your home in such location, with a master bedroom with views that allows you see the sunset into the tranquil wave of the sea. I am not sure anyone can definitely explain why this works, but it does, it has worked for all captain of industries, successful athletes and more.

Fourthly you have to begin acting in accordance with your vision. It is most certain that the super consciousness will begin the creation of what you have asked for, as long as you believe. However, in order to receive what you have asked for, you will need to take actions that are directly inspired by your vision. It is only by doing so, are you able to receive what you have asked for. This is a very important step to the process of being successful with your online business. Most people learn what to do, but it is ever more important to do the things required with the right energy and intensity. The intensity is not necessarily quantifiable, but makes a substantial difference to the outcome you get in running a successful online business.

In addition, you have to be willing to give what it takes to get what you are after. In as much as you have accepted that you need to take actions that are aligned to what you want, you really have to do the actions whatever they may be to such a level that there is no doubt, that you really want what you are asking for. This will bring the sort of intensity that is required to get anything worth having.

Finally once you get what you are after, you need to appreciate them for what there are and express your gratitude to the super consciousness for granting your wishes. This will mean you can get even more things when you next ask for them. You find some people unhappy in spite of wealth, and this may be one reason why, a lack of appreciation.

I reflected whether to provide the steps outlined so far, in the introduction of a book about becoming rich through your online business. However, the feeling I have, is the book exists to aid you with your goal of succeeding in your online business. As such, it would be unfortunate if I did not provide a process of thinking and acting, that would steer you on the right path to achieving your aim of making money with your online business.

2 GOALS MAKE YOU RICH

Ever wondered what the likes of Bill Gates, Andrew Carnegie, Tom Watson and Steve Jobs have in common. They all had a vision and goals to match. Bill Gate is reputed to have held a vision of every household with a PC. Selling his software to them made him billions. Tom Watson of IBM had a clear vision of what IBM would look like before he got there. To be rich online you need to start with a vision and goals to match.

Yet in spite what experience shows is the need for a vision and goals. The reality is that most start their online businesses without clear goals. The result is a predictable state of confusion and spinning of wheels. Since the intention is to stack the cards in your favor, in order that you make money. This chapter strive to show you how goals make you rich, to keep you focused on the price.

Just as important, is to heed those words of wisdom, succinctly put by that famous English poet William Ernest Henley. "I am the Master of my fate, the Captain of my soul". My overarching strive, is to empower you with all the knowledge required for success online. In order that you be able to exercise to the fullest, that inalienable rights to freedom and self determination. With this in mind, we begin the journey from the most important question of all.

What is Money?

So you want to start a business and you are probably investigating which opportunity would be most suited to your liking. Obviously the point of your quest is probably not solely to run an online business for it sake. But to make the sort of money that made Michael Douglas as Gordon Gekko state greed was good in the movie "Wall Street". Ok your thoughts may not be on this scale or motive, but you get the point.

Before you begin, have you taken a moment to ask yourself what money is? What exactly is this thing called money, and why do you need or want it so badly?

I want money, I don't need to know what it is you say. Well you did start by wanting to become your own banker remember. A little bit of insight into money will not go amiss.

The origin of money was due to the restriction of barter. It earliest form was in the form of precious metals like the bronze during roman times to gold in later days. To a certain extent the precious metals represented the labor required in producing them. Just like barter before it, which was based on the exchange of goods which in turn represented the labor used in producing them.

In order to safeguard their gold for future use, people began seeking location for which to store them. They found goldsmiths to be ideal in fulfilling this need. As part of the safekeeping of gold, the goldsmith in turn issue notes indicative of the gold stored.

No sooner the issued notes, became acceptable as a pseudo legal tender. And the goldsmiths found at a given time a high proportion of the notes were not redeemed. Hence, they saw an opportunity in loaning gold and making money on the interest.

This formed the basis of our modern day monetary system. The difference is that the central bank prints the gold, and the commercial banks create and expand the monetary pool. Which means the restriction of gold is removed, and to all intent increasing supply of money attainable, as wealth increases.

So the money in of itself is not what you are after. You are instead after a portion of the labor force through your resourcefulness. And what that portion of the labor force, which is the wealth within the society (including land) is able to get for you in return. We are in unique times today, as the internet breaks societal boundaries, and allows us to tap into wealth in other society. A truly magnificent treasure when you know how to access it.

How To Get Money

The next important question is how you get money. The answer to this is quite simple. You can get money through the transfer of wealth from those that have it to yourself. Or you can get money through the addition to the collective wealth, of society.

Digressing ever so slightly, both ways of getting money have significant differences. One approach see wealth as limited and as such to get it one has to replace others with wealth. The other sees wealth as ever increasing, and as such to get it you only need to look to add to the wealth available through your online business, and as such rewarded for doing so.

Thus, how you choose to pursue money matters with regards to the culture of your online business. A personal approach of mine is to view my online business as a way of adding to the wealth of the online industry, through innovative and improved ways of doing business. This means competitors are not necessarily enemies of mine to be vanquished. Instead my aim is to increase value. In some instances, collaboration with competitors may be required.

However, if as a result of the value you add, you trump competitors, that should be seen as just a side effect of the game and not the aim. I will discuss more on this in subsequent chapter.

Getting back to the business of making money, as you can see from our discussion so far, no one really needs money for money sake. The reasons you think you need money are for the things you can get with it. So it stands to reason, that the more reasons you have for wanting those things which money gives you, the more likely you are to attaining your wishes of making money though your online business.

We now have our reasons lets go on our treasure hunt. Stop for a second where is our treasure map? Why do we need one. I hear the treasure is somewhere in Peru. With luck once we get there we will track down the treasure cave. I also hear the cave is packed with gold and diamonds beyond imagination.

Hold on a second we can't go on such a potential profitable expedition, full of all sort of danger and exciting distractions, without a map of the exact location of the cave. And why do we need all that diamond anyway, I hear the route is full of all sort of obstacles. Simple I want to be rich! What does this mean. Ok then to be financially independent! How do you mean. And so the story goes.

I hope you see the relevance of the story just told regarding setting goals and putting together a map to your online riches. You may have previously viewed goal setting exercise as unnecessary. But the reality is simple if you are not clear on your goals, you will make no money online. Very rarely do people make money accidently, they do so through deliberate efforts, which begins from goal setting.

In order to help your treasure hunt, I have provided you with a typical list of why some may need money. I suggest you use this and make a personal list. I mean putting it in writing and picturing every goal in your mind. The key is to feel these goals emotionally, which in turn should create the impulse to go after them. If these are things you really want, then creating the feeling required to push you to get them, should come naturally.

Typical Reasons For Wanting Money

- You may like to have a house similar to those own by movie stars.

- You may like to put together an education fund fit for the next Estienne.

- Retirement funds is short and you may want to build for retirement, in order to maintain the serene life you dream of.

- How about that car, the one fit for an executive.

- You may just want to go on holidays to nice places, south of France is probably a destination of choice.

- You may just need to build a savings fund for a rainy day, or can never be too careful.

- You may have just experience a changed in personal circumstance that requires some money

- Need to pay all manners of bills
- Need an extra income and more.

The aim is to prevent the last three listed goals, if they are applicable and aspire for the others.

The more you have on your personal wish list, and the more you make them personal, the more you are able envision what you want in your mind, the better motivated you will be in pursuing your goal of making money. The goals should all fit into a sort of life style vision for yourself. Make sure once you have built this vision in your mind you hold on to it henceforth.

Once you have decided on the reasons for which money is required. The next question to ask yourself, would be how much money is needed to sustain the lifestyle you hope to live. Would the lifestyle of Trump be ok, or that of your average plastic surgeon.

You really should think carefully about this, and try not to come up with off the cuff answers like "as much as possible", or "only to pay the bills" etc. What is required is to take your personal wish list and convert them into goals that are specific with deadlines for when you hope to accomplish them. Think of them as money in the bank on route to an accomplished life. As an example I have taken some element of the typical wish list provided previously and turned them into goals with deadlines below:

Goal	Amount Required	Date
Need to buy a dream Home	$300,000	31st December 2012
Need to buy a car	$40,000	1st March 2011

Once you have converted your personal wish list into goals with deadlines as I have shown above, you will then need to develop your own personal income statement. Remember, the notion of reading the map on route to your destination, requires a knowledge of your present condition, which your income statement embodies. Suffice to say, I am often reminded of the saying- "for you to know where you are going to, you must know where you have been".

Your income statement mainly covers your income and expenses within a specified duration. Being that we are talking about a personal income statement, a suitable duration to capture would be your monthly income and expenses. I know this task sounds boring. However it is most beneficial to your ultimate goal of making money online, so I seriously recommend you do not skip this, and get one done at some point. Here is a template of an income statement you could use.

Category	Monthly Amount	Net Profit/ Loss
Income		
		Total income
Expenses		
		Total Expenses

Once you have worked out your personal wish list which mainly captures your monetary goals, and you have done an income statement which captures your present financial condition. You are now in a position to use both items to work out what your overall financial goal will need to be to provide for your financial security.

This final list which I like to refer to as the "list of becoming", should show how much you need yearly, monthly and daily, to fulfill the goals you have outlined. This list should become the list for which your online business is used to fulfill your aim of making money.

In a nutshell the goals should allow you to make sound choices from the plethora of online businesses. Because you are now able to pick those business that are viable enough in supporting your personal objectives. Remember this process is flexible and iterative, and can be updated as you become more knowledgeable on what's required.

In addition to your financial goals, there are usually other reasons not necessarily financial, which you may have, that have led to your seeking a business opportunity online. Some of these reasons may be as follows:

- You have probably come to the end of your tether, with your boss. And the notion of becoming your own boss is most appealing.
- May be you are at a point, where personal circumstance means you need flexible working hours, which you are hoping to achieve through your business.
- You may just like to do what you enjoy doing through business. A sort of living your own life and dreams
- You want a sense of achievement and recognition that comes with running a successful business.
- Or you are tired of the travelling involved with your current work and more.

Put them down as add-on to your list of becoming. The benefit of doing so, is to inspire you alongside your monetary goals, to press on and attain them through your business.

You may still wonder what all this have to do with finding an online business. If that still be the case, spare a thought for the aimless souls, that move from one online business opportunities to another. Not giving the required time needed for success in any. The biggest reason why about 90% of people looking to run a business online, fall into this trap, is based on not having clear goals. I can't stress enough how important this is to your success in making money online.

By now you have a clear financial goal, and your non monetary goals that will aid in guiding your choice from the range of online businesses available to you. The agenda is set and we can start digging for gold, with the same attitude General Patton had when he said "If you are going to win any battle, you have to do one thing. You have to make the mind run the body. Never let the body tell the mind what to do... the body is never tired if the mind is not tired."

3 DIG FOR GOLD

I am often reminded of the Gold rush of the 19th century that took place in California. As the story goes, gold was discovered by James Marshal and John Shutter. John wanted the lead kept on the discovery of gold, in order not to hinder plans he had for a business venture.

However as is always the case, when something good is found, Samuel Brannan a publisher, got wind of the story. It was said that he ran down the street with gold in his hands shouting "Gold! Gold! Gold from the American River!". And began the adventure of a lifetime, that lead many ordinary people to substantial wealth including making Brannan the richest man in California.

Interestingly, both Mr. Sutter and Mr. Marshal died broke, for whatever reason unknown to us today. It may very well be a headstrong refusal to make money the simple way. Or maybe the unpreparedness to seize the moment. It just shows the street might be paved with gold, and yet most may miss their chance of getting rich. A similar tale as told is unfolding today online.

Now it must be said just like the gold rush of yesteryear, one is unable to predict the exact amounts you will earn daily. Some days it may be at the upper end of you daily range, others the lower end. The point is no business can be 100% predictable. Then again the same applies to a job these days.

Actually some business are even more predictable than a job over the long run. And once you make your fortune who cares about the daily gyrations of earnings. I am sure Richard Branson of Virgin, is not pondering over earning a few million less in a month, or Bill Gates worried about being knocked off the richest list by Carlos Slim . Anyway I will show you how you can make your earnings more predictable in the subsequent chapters.

Why Online Business?

Your business is your vehicle to wealth, and the type of business you choose to run is important. There are broadly two choices to make here. Well three if you combine both as a choice. But we will stick with two. You have the old way, of starting a business, which effectively is based on the old bricks and mortar approach. These businesses are usually quite expensive to startup, potentially restricted by geography and all other manners of limitations. Because of this, the chances of success are reduced depending on the market you go for.

On the other hand, the new approach which leverages the inter connectivity of the internet, to make substantial income, is relatively flexible, cheap to start-up, less effort needed to start with, and in most cases, once setup a big part of the business can be automated, freeing you to think up other ways of making even more money. Right now they are a number of genuine people, from humble beginnings, using the internet to make substantial incomes online. There is no reason why you can't be one of them.

In order to make money online, you need to accept all for profit businesses, solely exist to serve groups of customers or markets. So if you want to make a fortune, you need to focus your attention, on helping a group of individuals, in an area of interest, preferably one that needs solutions to problems.

Since this book is mainly focused on online businesses, my advice would be centered on how to look for group of customers online. Which you can then proceed to serve profitably. Nonetheless, in as much as the focus is on online businesses, the principles are applicable to offline businesses as well. The same skills developed, are transferable between online to offline, and vice versa. In the end all businesses are really all about finding and serving their customers profitably.

This is why the first lesson for detecting scams online is quite simple. If it is masqueraded as a genuine business, then it must have genuine customers for which it exist to serve. Look into the customers and see if they really do exist and if they demand what is offered before getting into any dealings with anyone offering some auto pilot system that will make you millions online.

This is apart from the fact, that anyone offering an extremely unrealistic way of making money online is most likely misstating the facts and should not be trusted. Starting and running an online business requires time and effort to be successful, and the sooner people refuse to fall prey to unrealistic claims the better the standing of the industry. Take your time enjoy and master the process, which is repeatable and able to make you more money.

Once you are able to bust scams out there, the next step would be to find a legitimate online business that will make you money. The reality, is that there are numerous ways of making money online as of the time of writing. There is a further flux of additional ways of making money online, that gets unraveled daily. Making the choice of picking the right business potentially complicated.

This has led many to a form of decision paralysis in making the right choices, due to the constant barrage of over information. It is important to understand, that the internet, albeit a great invention for its global reach. Is just another distribution channel.

Just like direct mail before it, telesales, door to door sales, you name it, it is just a way of reaching your potential customers. Obviously with potential for making more people rich, simply because of its global scale. And so, the sooner one understands that it is really a distribution channel, the better one becomes at screening the noise that comes with the jargons and flux associated with online businesses.

Thus allowing you to focus on what is important in starting your online business. The biggest misunderstanding, is that all the various ways for making money online, are the most import elements to consider. As important as there are, what really matters the most is you and you take precedence over everything else.

To begin the research required for your online business, you need to understand how your potential customers use the internet for their needs. This is a gold mine and should be followed diligently. What is even better, is you do not have to be like those alchemist looking for that elusive germ the "philosopher stone". What you seek is right in front of you and begins with your understanding of the behavior of your potential customer.

Interestingly, the process has been made easier by the evolution of the internet. The internet original purpose was a place for customers to find information, and this approach still exist today.

However, it has now evolved to one that also offers a medium for customers to meet other customers. This setup provides your online business with the opportunity to be reached by prospective customers, and for your online business to also use the mechanism to reach your customers. But before all this, what is even more unique, is the wealth of information provided. Which allows you to easily determine the feasibility for making money through a particular project. Let see how this is done.

The Steps to Starting An Online Business are as follows (Formulating Your Business Idea)

You will notice by now, that I am all for making as much money as you can. In fact I am a champion of this course, and of living a complete life. This is the reason this book was written, to take as many people out of a struggling existence, by providing useable knowledge. So you will think I am all wholly focusing on just making money exclusion of other factors. To this I will say no, as a position of selfishness always nearly lead to ruin.

Most people come into the business of making money online with the sole focus of only wanting to know how to make money quickly. To be honest they are probably not after the process, they only want the end result right now. In some instance if you are able to produce a magic wand to achieve this even better.

This fundamental error leads them to a point of desperation which in turn leads them to making avoidable mistakes with starting their businesses online. They do not realize that in as much as it is the purpose of their business, to make money online, in reality they will only achieve this aim, if they focus their energy on providing needed service. Before you get the gold, you have to dig for it. You cannot get the gold in without the required mining service.

Hence, the first step required to starting your business online, is to focus on the market you intend to serve as a potential owner of an online business. This is a very important point that cannot be overstated, and you will do well to use as a solid foundation, for which to build your business online. The basic point addressed here, is for you to formulate an idea associated with serving a market which will drive your overall business agenda.

There are times when some just starting out, do not know enough to be sure of an idea to pursue online. If this is the case, do not worry, as it has its advantages one of them being that you have no preconception, and as such able to treat the idea of running an online business as a clean canvas. To get the ball rolling, look at starting your business from the premise, that you will increase your probability of success, doing what you are most predisposed to do.

Yet, at times, it is not necessarily clear to some, what they are most predisposed to do. In order to help, I will assume that since you are reading this book, you already know that you would like to run a form of business online, and you are only looking for guidance on what business will be most suitable for you.

All businesses are based on selling to customers. Some people are better at selling and marketing tangible products like houses, cars etc, while others are better at selling and marketing intangibles like services, information products etc. As an example, if you are interested in the esoteric aspect of life, that is you are more interested in abstract concepts and ideas, then it is quite likely that you are better predisposed to selling and marketing intangibles.

On the other hand those more interested in exoteric aspects of life, those that prefer the touch and feel of what they sell, are quite likely predisposed to selling tangibles. Knowing which group you fall into is very important in been able to decide which of the many businesses online is suitable to you. It will save you wasted time and effort, as you are less likely to be successfully running a business not aligned to your values.

Once you understand what type of products/services, you are most predisposed to offering through your business, the next step is to decide on the type of market to get into. If you have a skill or product knowledge within a specific niche of interest, look to base your business around this area. The reason for this, is it gives you a very good chance of succeeding online. For example you can offer various consulting services through your online business. Thus if you know what business to get into, then your initial challenge may be in knowing the steps required in performing a niche research online which will be discussed in this chapter.

However, for those who now know the sort of business they are better predisposed to running, but still not sure on the exact business to run online, you will need to put in some work to get to that point. Look to identify a market that is hungry for something and then look to provide what they are hungry for.

The way to do this online is to start your research using the search engine. As of the time of writing Google is the biggest by far of all search engines, and as such the one I will be using to show you how to find and research niche markets. Even if you already know what you intend doing online, you can still use these steps to verify that your target market has adequate demand for your business.

Finding Niche Market

The first thing you would have noticed is my approach in focusing on finding a niche to serve and not a product to sell. This is very important, as the right niche pays your income online, and if you get a hungry niche with money to spend, you can continuously serve that niche and get paid for doing so, regardless of products.

Most newbie do this the wrong way round, as they find a product and then try and form a business, around that product and fail at the first hurdle. Another advantage of looking for the niche to serve is the fact that most times, a niche requires more than one product. This allows you to diversify your income stream by focusing on the market and providing multiple products instead of the focus on products as most do. Products may go out of fashion and you are left to start all over again looking for products to sell.

Characteristics Of A Good Niche

In order that you find a profitable niche, you will need to know what to look for in a niche. Hence it is important we identify those characteristics, that make for a successful niche. This will then encourage you to start your business, on solid ground, full of confidence that you will make money. Here are the characteristics to look for:

1. The niche should be large enough online, that is there are a reasonable number of people actively looking for solutions within the niche.
2. The niche is not heavily dependent on price i.e. niche members will put value over price when making buying decisions.
3. The niche is not crowded with big brand names as this will make it very difficult although not impossible to compete in.
4. The market is supplied by businesses that are not providing the right solutions efficiently, or have not kept themselves up to date with the niche demand.

No one expects that you will have all the characteristics mentioned above in a niche of your choice. Nevertheless, the more you have these characteristics in your niche the more chances you have of success in your online business.

Online Market Research

Most traffic i.e. potential customers likely to visit your online business, are going to come from people looking for what you provide. They do this mainly through search engines, which then attempts to match the information required online, in this case your business offerings, to the request provided by a potential customer.

Thus your job in starting a business online will be to investigate the needs of the customers, who are using the search engines to find solutions to their problems. This is especially true, if you have no idea on what business to start online. Because Google has about 70% of these searches, we look to use Google as a starting point in understanding what our potential customers are looking for online.

It is important not to get bogged down with the fact that Google is used in this instance to begin the research. If in ten years time your customers uses some other means of finding solutions to their problems, that should not negate the skills you acquire here.

This is because the principle, remains the same and it is quite simple. You always start your research where most customers go to look for solutions. Technology has made this process easier and will continue to make it so. So do not be too worried about your skills being obsolete. Your potential customers will always converge in certain places on route to finding solutions to their problem. This is always going to be the case, based on our understanding of human nature.

Getting back to starting your online market research, the way you find out what information Google has, regarding online searches, in order that you begin to understand the customer needs, is by using a Google tool called the keyword tool. You can locate this tool, by simply typing the word "keyword tool" in the Google search column.

You will get the following screen capture as a result:

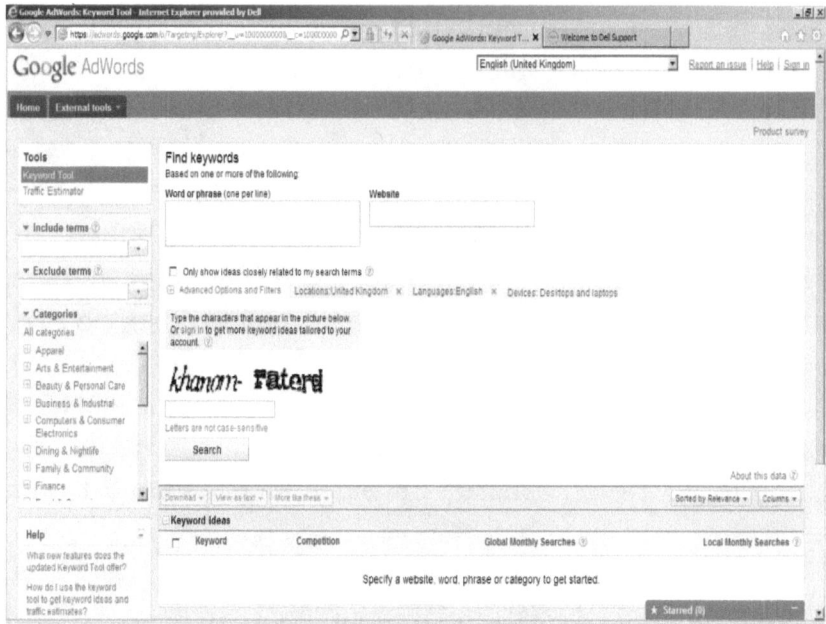

The keyword tool is a subset of the Google Adword setup(I will talk about Adword in the next chapter). You can use the tool without a Google Adword account, but you will only get limited information from the tool. In order that you get more information out of the keyword tool, you will need to create a free Google Adword account. You do this from the webpage shown clicking the "Sign in" link at the top right of the page, and creating an account from the subsequent page.

Since you are looking for a niche to serve, a starting point would be to think of words people may use when looking for solutions. I call them trigger words, and here are some examples of such words:

- Tips
- Buy
- Help
- How To
- Advice
- Prevent

The aim of this exercise is to find as many of these words as you can, to begin researching what people are looking for online. As a starter I will look to use the "tips" keyword on the keyword tool to see what comes out of the Google database to begin the research. See the next screen shot for output using the trigger word tips.

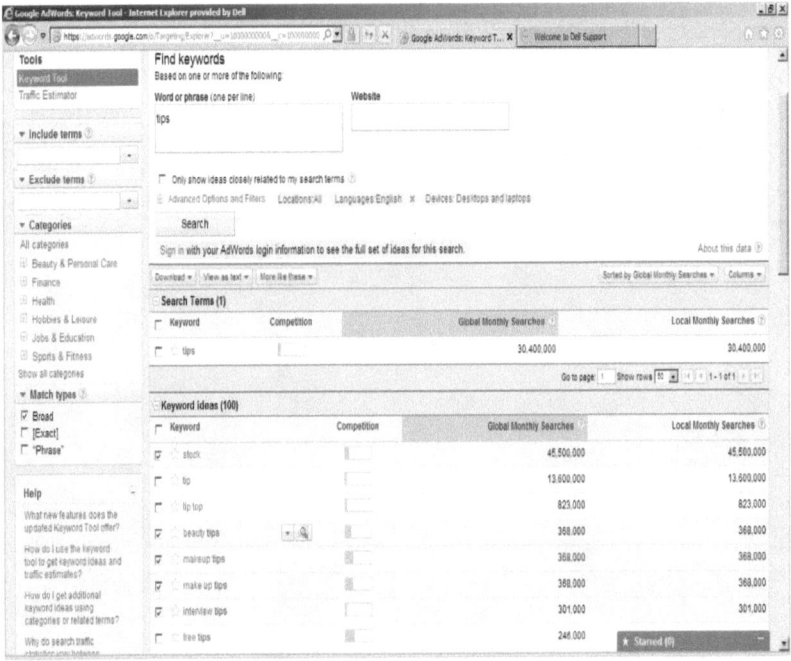

The screen above shows the output as a result of using the "tips" keyword on the Google Keyword tool. I have selected some interesting potential niches to investigate, one of them being "beauty tips", which I have chosen to begin my initial investigation. One of the reason for selecting this niche is due in part to the size of the search volume indicated under the "Global Monthly search" and "Local Month Searches" column, which is indicative of demand.

In addition, to the potential demand of the niche, another selection criterion, involves an assessment of the competition within the niche. On observation, if you look under the competition column for the "beauty tips" niche, you will find very little competition for the niche. This bodes well for your potential online business.

We now look to investigate "beauty tips" niche further, by entering the keyword into Google. I have so far used the word "keyword" without initially explaining what these are. There are simply any word used by your potential customers to search for information on a search engine.

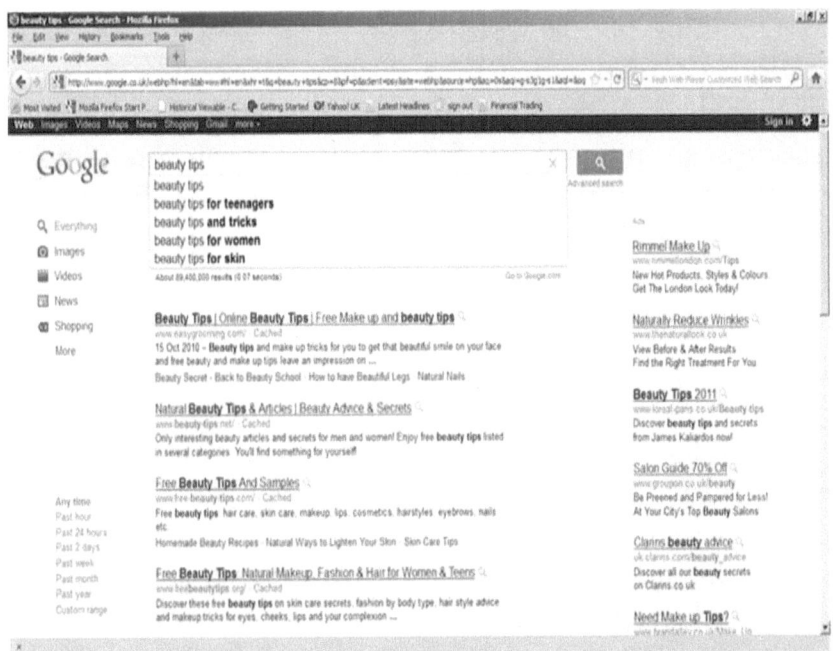

On entering the "beauty tips" keyword we make a number of interesting observations. One is to do with the alternative phrases you get below the beauty tip search. These phrases can be viewed as sub niches that we may want to exploit within the "beauty tip", niche as part of our strategy. Again it will all depend on demand and competition within these sub niches.

The other observation we make, is that there is a healthy number of paid or sponsored ads on the right side of the page, which is indicative of a healthy demand for the "beauty tip" niche.

The next step in the research is for you to open up the top three websites found by Google for the "beauty tips" niche and study their contents. The way to do this is to make note

35

of the titles of the websites and the titles of the various sections covered within the websites. The aim here, is to get an initial understanding of the needs addressed by the businesses running these sites. This is to give you a first take on the potential problems being faced by customers and how there are being addressed by competitors within the niche. Also in some instances studying the websites within the niche provides a bit more information on the type of customers served by that niche.

On initial study of the website listed by Google, the information provided by these sites deal with hair, skin, body and makeup for face, eyes and lips, with a general dose of beauty advice. The target market addressed are women and young girls,. They are looking for solutions to their needs for looking and feeling good. And the websites attempts to address this needs by providing them with information, products and services. The core essence is to help provide for their need to look and feel secured in their appearance. See appendix A.1 for screen capture of these potential competitor websites.

Beyond the initial study of the website found. You will also need to enter the web addresses for each of the top three sites listed by Google, into the keyword tool. You do this with the box that has "website" as its title on the keyword tool page. See an example of me entering the web address for the top search on Google on the next screen shot.

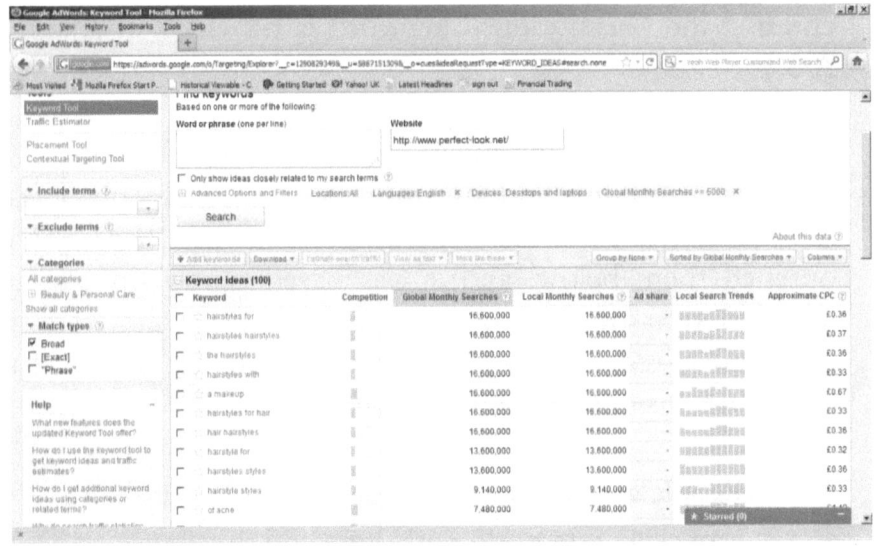

What is interesting, regarding this screen shot is that you can instantly see what keywords are used to locate the top sites within the "beauty tip" niche. The keywords found at this stage of the research should be saved somewhere on your computer, to be used later to compliment your research. It can also be used to setup advertising campaign on Google, which we will discuss in the next chapter.

See appendix A.2, A.3, A.4 for the output returned for each sites entered into the keyword tool. It is worth mentioning, that the "beauty tip" niche, may be too broad a niche for you to start with, so you may need to narrow your market within a sub niche of the "beauty tip" niche. This is similar to the market segmentation process you will normally go through, for an offline business.

For now, we will continue our work on the "beauty tips" niche, by carry on our research using "beauty tips" within the keyword tool, to see what other related keywords comes out of the Google search database. The output produced by entering the "beauty tips" keyword is provided in appendix A.5.

Go through the output in appendix A.2,A.3,A.4 and A.5 in order to understand my interpretation and how I have arrived at some of the conclusions provided here. I have outlined them below, and it was based purely on a simple interpretation of the keywords produced so far from the research. It really is nothing fanciful. Here are some of the initial conclusions drawn from the data:

- People are looking for solutions to skin problem especially one to do with acne and dry skin.
- People are looking for solutions to hair problem, for example hair styles, and hair loss problem.
- People are looking to stay young by reducing wrinkles and eliminating stretch marks.
- People are looking for ways to look good for their wedding day.

These are important findings and will drive your agenda for setting up a business on online. Write them down, in your planning document, and carry on with the research.

The next phase of our research will be to use a powerful tool provided by Google called Google trend http://www.google.com/trends for further analysis. This is to make sure the demand for the niche has being in existence for a while. The reason we look for this, is to make sure we go into business, in niches that has proven themselves over a reasonable period. Niches with stable demand, as provided by Google trend confirms this notion.

On Review, of the output of Google trend for "beauty tips" niche, we get a picture of a stable demand for "beauty tips" over a reasonable period of time. This should bode well for making money through our online business.

Beyond the demand assessment, which we can see for "beauty tip" has been healthy. Another interesting observation we make, is one that shows the source of demand by countries. This may be an important factor to bear in mind when choosing a niche. And as such knowing this gives you more insight into your potential niche market. In addition knowing what regions or countries demands your product or services, allow you to target your ads effectively if using Google.

The next thing you want to do is to find out where your potential customers go to online, i.e. blogs and forum, and investigate what their problems are in more detail. You can think of blogs and forums as a place where like minded people converge and discuss issues of importance, sort of an online private club.

As of the time of writing, the top two search sites used for finding blogs are:
- Technorati: http://technorati.com/
- Google: http://blogsearch.google.com/

In the case of technorati, it also rates the blogs within your niche.

To begin this phase of the research, you simply enter the "beauty tips" keyword in the mentioned search site, and review the first few blogs that appear from the search. What you are looking for, are the titles of the blogs, and the topics discussed on these blogs in order to further understand some of the problems faced by the "beauty tips" niche. See Appendix A.6 for details of some of the blogs found for beauty tips. The general theme garnered from these blogs, is on par with what was delineated from the keyword research phase.

Further investigation is also carried out through forums, which you can find by repeating the process of entering the "beauty tips" keyword in the sites listed below, which as of the time of writing are the top three sites focused on tracking forums.

- Boardreader: http://boardreader.com/
- Omgili: http://omgili.com/
- Boardtracker: http://www.boardtracker.com/.

Look to read what problems your prospective customers are faced with and think about how you can help them solve their problems. On review, the forum corroborates some of the findings found with the keyword research section. However, it also provides deeper insight, on the challenges faced by the niche, with skin care problems to do with acne, ageing, dryness and lighten requiring the most solutions from potential customers. See Appendix A.7 for details of some of the forums found for beauty tips

Carry out additional research on popular ecommerce sites like Amazon and eBay, by following the same process used to research the niche via Google, the blogs and forum. When you are doing this on eBay use their free research tool eBay Pulse for your research located here http://pulse.ebay.com/.

On reviewing the Beauty and Health categories on eBay, it shows up the popular searches for this niche. An interesting product "Mary Kay" which also appears high-up the Google keyword research data (which you can verify in appendix

A.5), also appears on the top ten list. You can also see some of the biggest shops in that niche on eBay. Look at what this potential competitors are doing.

See next a screen capture of what I am referring to.

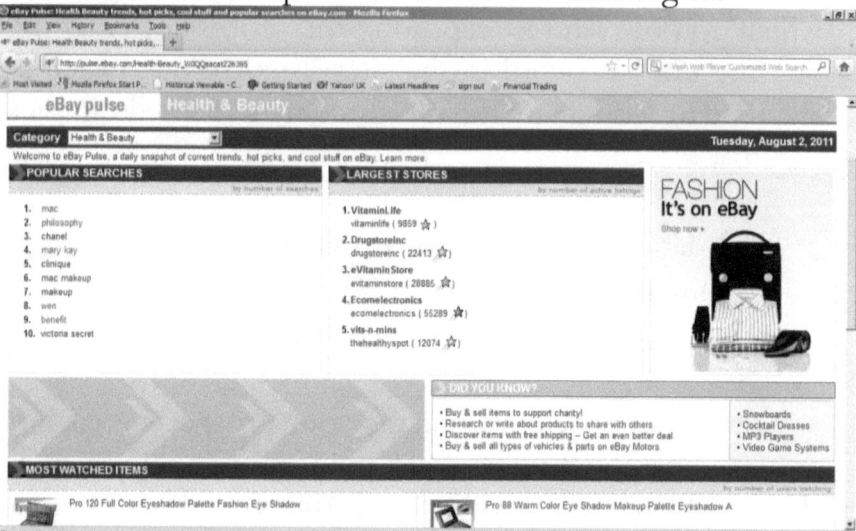

Further research on Amazon shows crucial beauty trends and a converges of demand for certain products seen with Google keyword research and eBay. See next screen shots for details.

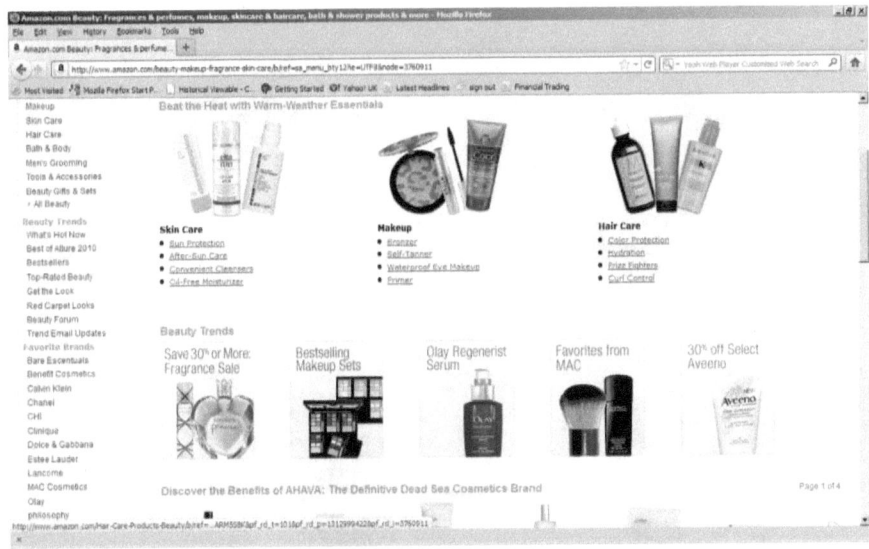

You can also use a number of "How to" sites to aid your research. These sites provides books and articles and videos on how to do things. Entries on the site are a measure of demand and should be added to your research. The two popular ones are
http://www.ehow.com/
http://www.howtodothings.com/.

The next screen shot shows what is of demand on the eHow Site.

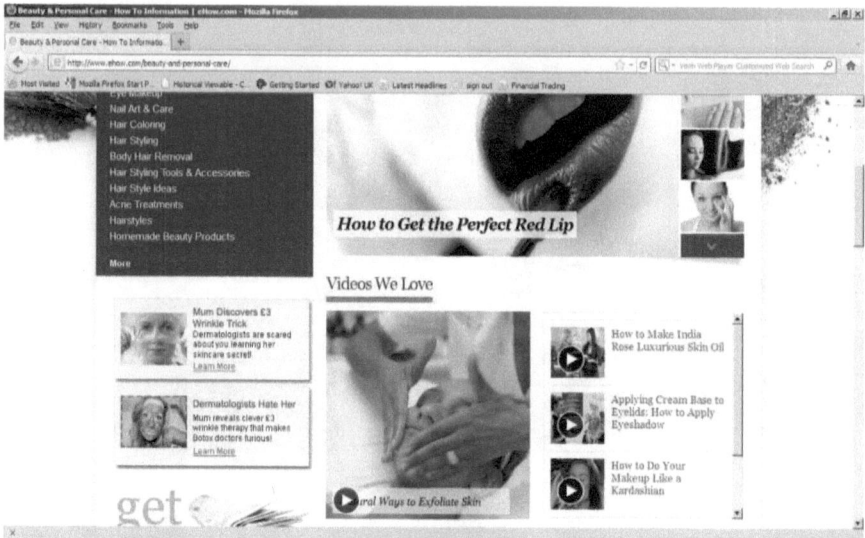

You can also supplement your research by reading magazines on beauty tips for example, go to various shops and see how many magazines they have stalked on their shelves. The more magazines there have up, the more indication of demand. The same applies to books as well. Research their titles, what are the common problems discussed and how if at all are there addressed.

There really are benefits in doing some offline research, because these days the online and offline world are becoming more converged. The more you know about your customer and the more you understand their problems the better you are able to serve their needs which equates to more money to you through your online business. However avoid the ills of paralysis from analysis, at some point you really would have to test the market to be sure of the research carried out.

Strengths, Weaknesses, Opportunities, Threats (SWOT)

This phase should guide your decision on the most appropriate online business that would match your needs. As a new business the SWOT should be based on you, any management team involved in the running of the online business, and your chosen niche.

See below for a template you can use to accomplish your SWOT analysis for your chosen niche I have given example, but do not limit yourself to them. The supreme aim is to allow you to understand your strength and opportunities, that will serve as good competitive advantage for your online business, if properly understood. And to understand any potential threat, and weakness, which you can mitigate for.

SWOT TEMPLATE FOR STARTING ONLINE BUSINESS

Strength	Examples You Can Look at for Reference
	What are your Capabilities? Can you work long hours, are you persistent, do you have stamina
	What are your Competitive advantages? Is it based on innovative delivery of customer needs, customer care, a genuine gap in the market etc
	What are the advantages of your business?
	What is your knowledge and experience? Do you have experience of the market, do you have a partner that has experience of the market, are you a quick learner, etc
	What are your financial resources like? Do you have some resource to allow you cope with the

	initial months of stating your online business?
	What are your Philosophy and values? Can there be viewed as strength to your online business.
	Are you a survivor? Are you one that commits to succeed at any cost?
	How is your health?

Weakness	Examples You Can Look at for Reference
	What are the gaps in your Capabilities?
	What is your lack of competitive strength?
	What are the disadvantages of your business?
	What are your gaps in sales and marketing?
	What are your gaps in financial resources? E.g. cash flow funds, start-up funds
	What are your personal weaknesses?
	Where are your gaps in reputation within the market?
	How is your health?

Opportunities	Examples You Can Look at for Reference
	What are the current developments in your Market that may give rise to opportunities?

	What are the weaknesses of your Competitors' you could use to your own advantage?
	What are the current lifestyle trends that may create additional opportunities?
	What are the technological development and innovation?
	What are the global influences that will provide opportunities?

Threats	Examples You Can Look at for Reference
	What are the Political changes that may impact your online business?
	What are the regulations that may impact your online business?
	What is your competitor intention that may impact your advantage?
	What is the trend in Market demand?
	What are the new technologies, services that may erode you online business model?

This chapter shows how much you can learn on any niche by doing your research. When I started this book, I did not know much about the beauty niche. Nonetheless, by simply going through the research, I have acquired a reasonable knowledge of the products/services, competitors and overall structure of the niche. It just shows what is possible with the volume of information out there. My advice would be to always carry out simple research before starting your online business.

Carrying out the research required for the success of your business should be fun. If it feels like a chore, then think seriously about the niche you are intending to go into, as this may be a sign that you are probably not picking the right niche aligned to your values. The SWOT if carried out properly should show you areas where you are good at, and opportunities you can take advantage of, through your online business.

Do not let whatever weakness you uncover to discourage you, most can be dealt with, with the right training, determination, perseverance. I always reminded by what Maggie Mason founder of Mighty Goods once said "Don't ever let anyone tell you that something is too competitive. Once you subtract the people who don't work very hard, or the people who aren't as good as you, your competition shrinks dramatically."

4 BECOME FAMOUS THROUGH YOUR ONLINE BUSINESS

To become famous may not be a direct ambition of yours. But its pecks and rewards are great to have. Who wouldn't want to attend exclusive events also attended by others you admire and respect. To wine and dine with royalty and be the envy of others. Most wouldn't mind that, and so does your business.

One of the most famous business I know of is Coca-cola. Would you believe it, when Mr. John Stith Pemberton developed the famous recipe, it was simply a patent medicine. I am not sure he had a global company in mind. It was Mr. Asa Griggs Candler, who bought a stake in the company, and applied aggressive marketing tactics, which brought about the multibillion dollar company we see today. The brand is now interwoven into the psyche of society. Another individual of our time, that embodies this concept is Mr. Trump. He lives through his business, his brand inspires success.

You may not get your business to be as popular as coke, or that of Trump. But the right advertising and marketing will make your business rich and famous. You are the biggest mouthpiece there is for your business. Be different infuse your business with your identity. Ok let's see how you too can get that megaphone out, and project your online business to the stratosphere.

The Marketing and Advertising of your online business

At this juncture, you have now worked out your financial goals, done your niche research, and come up with an idea for a business. The next thing for you to do, will be to understand the type of businesses available to you online, and how to go about advertising and marketing your chosen online business. The fact is if you do not let people know about your online business, then you really have no business, hence it is imperative to the success of your online business to make it known.

In addition to understanding what's required to making your business known online, it is important to also work out how to best serve your niche or customers through your online business. Thus I have provided some of the online businesses you can setup and run for the purpose of serving your niche as follows:

Affiliate Marketing/Sales Business

If you have ever come across agents offline whose main function is to market and sell products of other businesses, but aren't necessarily employees of these businesses. But are instead in business on their own, that is what an affiliate is online. He or she would promote one or more products from one or more businesses to their niche. Just like agents offline, they get paid commissions to sell products for which they promote.

The advantage of running an affiliate business is that you don't even need a website to start. All you need to do is to promote the websites offering the products of other businesses to your niche. The advantage for the businesses operating an affiliate program is that the cost of promoting and marketing the product is passed on to the affiliate. Obviously there is still an element of cost incurred by the business/vendor, which is the commission paid to the affiliate. The disadvantage of an affiliate program to an affiliate, is the lack of control over the product, including its listing price, and the actual sales pitch used in selling the product.

I have outlined below, some of the ways your online business may get paid on affiliate programs.

One Tier Affiliate Program

This is more or less your standard affiliate program I previously described. You get paid a commission on the actual sales you bring into the business. As an example, a company offers an affiliate program for which affiliates get 50% commission. This means if their product has a listing price of $150 you get $75 as commission for making a sale and that's it.

Two Tier Affiliate Program

A Two tier affiliate program on the other hand, pays commissions based on two levels. It has a Multi level or network marketing twist to it. You are not only selling the actual products, but also recruiting other affiliates to the company. Thus what happens is unlike the one tier program where affiliates only get paid once for selling the products.

With the two tier programs, affiliates receive a commission for each sale they make and for each sale their affiliate recruits make as well. This provides an incentive for recruiting other affiliates to the program. If we go back to our previous example of $150 sale for the product, if you made a sale, and the affiliate you recruited made a similar sale, not only will you be receiving your standard commission for the sales you made, but you will also receive commission from the sales made by the affiliates you recruited.

Residual Affiliate Programs

As I have stated previously picking the right niche for any business you choose to setup online, is crucial to success online. However, beyond this I also mentioned that businesses online like any other business are unpredictable.

Nonetheless there is a way of adding some consistency to your affiliate business, that makes it less unpredictable. You achieve this, by promoting multiple affiliate programs that pay residual income. These programs are usually things like membership sites affiliate programs, newsletter subscription affiliate programs etc. The affiliate program pays you monthly, based on agreed commission for as long as the customer you bring in remains with the company. The more you get this sort of income for your affiliate business, the more peace of mind and predictability you put into your business.

Some of the popular sites that provide affiliate programs are Amazon, Clickbank, Commission Junction, Nerverblue and other established businesses online. They provide hundreds of affiliate products, and if your niche has any notable demand in it, you should find an affiliate program to match. To understand how to use the affiliate programs just mentioned, we take a look at one of them, to see if we have products that we could promote to the beauty niche.

I will use click bank, as an example of this. To begin, you will need to sign up for a free account. Once done, login and go to the "marketplace" section and look for your niche within the categories. In this case the beauty niche is under the "health and fitness" section. Once you get to the beauty niche section you will see a list of all the products available to be promoted to your niche. See an example of this on the next screen capture.

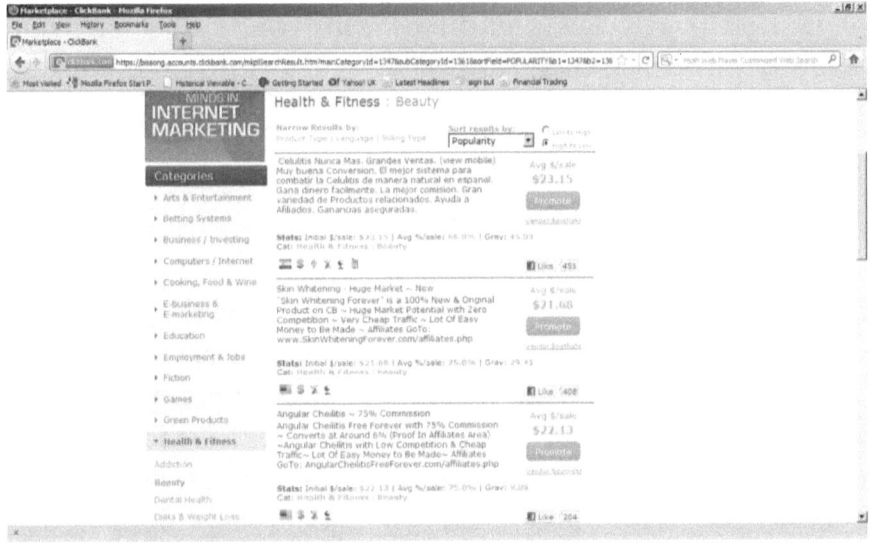

The average $/Sales tells you roughly how much you will earn per sale of the products. You should look to measure this figure against any advertising cost you may incur, as a result of promoting the product. This will determine your selecting the product to promote. In addition, clickbank has a unique way of tracking the success of sales for each products over a three months period. This tracking data is known as "gravity" and will be useful in your selection. As is a potential indication of demand for the product, within the niche.

Before you participate in any affiliate program make sure you read and understand the terms and conditions, review other people experiences with the program, understand the payment methods, how they deal with return goods and how that impacts your business. In addition, you want to make sure what they offer is of benefit to your niche. In some instance it may require you to test it out, and understand all the tracking in place for sales. You do all this to maintain and develop your reputation online with your customers, and to weed out any potential flawed affiliate program that may cause harm to your reputation.

Drop shipping Business

The drop shipping business is not too dissimilar to the affiliate sales business discussed previously. Apart from the fact that you are viewed as running a retailing business. As such you will require a website, to display the products you intend to sell to your customers. As the retailer you don't actually have to keep the goods you offer in stock. What you do, is to take the orders of the products required by your customers. You then transfer the orders and shipment details to either the manufacturer or the wholesaler of the products you display. There will then ship the goods directly to the customer on your behalf. As in any retail businesses, the online drop ship business makes money from the difference between the wholesale and retail price.

It is important you only deal with a genuine manufacturer or wholesaler, making sure you are buying wholesale price from them, in order to make money with the business. My advice here is to deal with legitimate businesses offline, that are happy to go in partnership with your online business. If you can, physically check them out and find out how many retailers, will be allowed into a drop shipping arrangement with them. This is because you are obviously thinking about competition which could eat up profit margin. In turn you will need to demonstrate why your online business should be taken seriously, and how much sales you see your business carrying out with them. Some of the information required will come from the research carried out on the niche.

Avoid majority of the online drop shipping companies, as most of them aren't wholesalers as claimed. But are simply retailers looking to set you up on a scam, by charging you near enough retail price with very little profit margin for your business. In some instance, they attempt to sell you readymade drop shipping websites, to sell these supposedly wholesale products. If you come across these lots, you should run a mile, as the chances of being landed with a turkey are extremely high.

The benefit you get from this business, is from doing the initial legwork required in establishing relationships with genuine wholesalers. This in turns reduces competition within your niche online. The reason for this, is because most people won't go the extra mile, and you win by doing just that. Make sure you understand the back end operations of the wholesalers you engage with, to reduce the chances of disappointment with delivery and inventory levels.

Pure Online Retail Stores

Like the other businesses discussed so far, it involves the buying and selling of products over the Internet using online shops. It in effect is a replica to an offline retail store, and includes the process of sourcing and stocking goods, marketing, selling, delivering, taking payments, servicing and after sales services. Items sold range from shoes, books, clothing, videos etc. The main difference between this form of business and the drop shipping form discussed previously, is that with this business, you will need to stock and mange the inventory of the products you sell online.

Some Business Ideas You Can Start With Today

Just in case you are still uncertain on what business to start online, or you are looking for specific ways of offering service to your niche, beyond the broad business type discussed so far. I have outlined a number of specific approaches you can take to start your online business today, and here there are:

1. You can start a business based on buying and selling websites. You may already have a niche. However, your preference may not be to serve the niche directly. Rather your preference may be to improve how the niche is served. You may look to achieve this objective by buying websites improving on them, and reselling them. As of the time of writing the number one site used for the buying and selling of websites is Flippa https://flippa.com/

2. You could look to write articles, make posts on forums and add entries in blogs, and get paid for offering these services. There are a number of websites that provide a gateway for you to use in offering these services. A simple search on Google or any other search engine, should bring up a list of these sites.

3. You could write and eBook on areas of interest with demand.

4. You could offer services like advertising, optimizing searches for customers and things that make businesses improve their web presence online.

You are limited on the type of business to run online, only by your imagination as there are constant opportunities to be of service online. Most businesses online will fall under the three broad types of business discussed so far. The key to establishing a successful online business is diversification of your income source.

Obviously when you start an online business, you should focus on one at most two niches and develop the business to the point where it is adequately profitable. Then look to increase your offerings to your niche, which would improve profitability and resilience of your online business.

Once you have got your business to this point, you can look to further expand your business by diversifying to other areas and income streams. By developing income from multiple sources, when one source is having a bad patch, you can supplement your income with the other source. But you have to do this intelligently as you can spread yourself too thin, if done incorrectly.

How To Reach Your Customers

In discussing how you are to reach your customers with solutions to their problems, our focus would be strictly limited to the use of the internet in reaching them. However if your home business allows for it, there is no need to limit your reach, to just the internet, you can look to use direct mail, telephone, and face to face to reach customers where possible, once you have verified your cost to profit ratio.

Coming back to the topic at hand, we need to answer the fundamental question of how one goes about reaching prospective customers. Before you attempt to do this, think through the research previously carried out, and attempt to fully articulate the challenges faced by your prospective customers. Then decide on what message you intend to convey about yourself and the products/service on offer, to which you propose as solutions to their problems.

Here is how the message you have for your customer should be structure

1. Any message you have for your prospective customer, should have a title or an opening that catches your prospects interest. Since you know a lot about your customer, this should not be too difficult to achieve. Put yourself in the customer shoes, before you begin the message. As an example, we know one of the problems faced by prospective customers, within the beauty niche, is one of skin care. This ranges from dry skin to acne. If you have a product that addresses this ills, you will look to put together a headline that focuses on the positive outcome of attain smooth beautiful skin free from acne, pimples, dry skins and oily ones. The essence is to get their attention with a positive interest.

2. Tell the customer about what your proposition is and how what you are proposing to them will solve his or her challenge.

3. Provide evidence if you can that the proposition you are offering them will solve their problem. This can be done in a number of ways. For example, you can offer the customer, testimonials of individuals that were in a

similar position to them and have since had their problems resolved by using your proposition. Better still get the customer to try it for themselves, to see how your proposition helps them. This depends on what you are offering, a little bit of creativity is needed on your part.

4. Make them aware of what they may miss out on, by not taking up your proposition. If your proposition is indeed able to provide for their pressing needs, then you do have an obligation to let them know what they may be missing out on, by not taking you up on the product/service on offer.

5. Tell them how to go about ordering the solution you provide for their problem.

The outline provided pretty much shows you how you should go about marketing and selling to your niche. Don't be fooled by some of the hype you see on the internet. To be successful in any online business you will need to develop your sales and marketing skills. If you are weak in these areas then you should seek some training to plug the gaps. If sales and marketing is not an interest of yours, then the only legitimate business I am aware of that does not require these skills, is stock trading or investing which I will be discussing in the final chapter.

How do you send the message to your customers?

There are various methods of doing this and it will mostly depend on your niche and the products/services on offer.

As an example, if you are looking to sell small ticket items, items of less than $50 then your preferred strategy may be spent on driving targeted traffic (online jargon for prospective customers) to the product and attempting to sell off the back of that traffic. On the other hand if you were selling big ticket item something above $500, then you may need a strategy that attempts to build your customer base and establish a relationship based on trust before providing them with the big ticket item.

However, regardless of the methods you use, you will need to attract traffic, and this begins the process of sending the message to your customers online. Before we discuss attracting traffic, you will need to have a website for which the traffic is directed to. If you are intending to run an online business with creditability then I suggest you do away with the option of running a free site under a sub domain of some other person's site. Look to purchase a domain from a domain provider, and look for a web hosting solution for your business site.

The sort of hosting package you go for will very much depend on the sort of business you intend to run, as an ecommerce site will have a different requirement to a pure information provision site. When looking for a host site, you have the option of getting one that gives you a web space and let you get on with building the site and loading it onto the space provided. This could be quite hands-on and will require some technical ability on your part. Or a requirement to outsource the building of your site to a website developer who will provide the technical skills needed to build the site. Your second option is to go with a host service that provides you with a range of website templates for you to use in putting your site together. This is relatively easy and good for those with limited technical skills.

However your control over the site is limited compared to the do it yourself option. In term of your choice think of a web site as you would a physical building, you don't find most offline businesses, especially small business owners, designing and building their premises. Sure you will have requirements of how you want your website to serve the needs of your customers, but my advice is to leave this aspect of your business to those who specialize in these services, and spend your time focused on developing your business, which ultimately are sales, marketing, product development and sourcing etc. I am not saying you should not take a keen interest on your website. It is very important to your business that you understand the technology that underpins your online business, that is why I have dedicated a chapter on technology in this book.

Nonetheless, what I am saying is for you to understand and manage the process of developing your website, without necessarily being bogged down with the technologies involved, especially if you have little or no technical background.

Marketing and Attracting Traffic

Getting back to the discussion of attracting traffic, as you would have seen from carrying out your research, there are millions of traffic online, and millions more are added each year. To attract targeted traffic from the millions online, you need to pay for it or put in the time and effort to get it.

Think about an offline business, how would you reach out to your customers? You may do the following:

- Distribute Brochures, leaflets and flyers
- Advertise in local papers and directories
- Advertise in special interest magazines
- Advertise in national newspaper and magazine
- Advertise on radio and TV
- Advertise in your local shops
- Word of mouth etc

The same process is required in letting your potential customers know you exist online and letting them know how to reach your business. As mention previously, there are pretty much two ways of attracting traffic to your website. One is based on paid advertising; the other unpaid advertising underpinned by your time and efforts.

Paid Advertising Model

There are a number of advertisers online that operate a number of pricing strategies that determines how you go about paying for advertising for your online business. Below are outlines of the various ways to do this online:

How Ads Is Paid

Cost-Per-Click (CPC) or Pay-Per-Click (PPC)

The first form of paid advertising discussed is the PPC. It works, by you placing an ad with an advertising provider, and you then pay the advertiser, each time someone clicks on the advert displayed. It is mainly operated by search engines operators like Google and Yahoo and so fits within a marketing strategy known as search engine marketing. However some social media networks like Facebook are also beginning to operate a similar PPC pricing model.

PPC is characterized, by you not paying the advertiser for the listing of your advert. You only pay when someone clicks on the listing. The most popular type of PPC are Google Adword , Yahoo Search Marketing and Facebook Ad. As of the time of writing Google Adword is the most popular of the three, and gives a good tutorial on how to use it.

However Facebook Ad is fast caching up, as companies are beginning to see the power of social media for highly targeted traffic.

In order to use these tools for example Google Adword, you need to make sure you are using the keywords you picked out during your niche research to better target your niche. In addition, you need to monitor and manage the ad campaign, or else they can become quite expensive and ineffective.

It is worth noting that under the Pay per click pricing system, using Google as an example, the more popular the keyword or niche the more expensive it is per click. In addition, you pay regardless of the fact that users could click and cancel before reaching your website.

Cost Per Action (CPA)

This is where your business only pays, when an action has occurred as a result of the advertising campaign. The action in question is agreed with the advertiser and it ranges from getting prospective clients to conduct an online survey, to actual buying of your product or services. When compared to PPC, it is actually less risky for your online business. The advertising is purely performance based, which means the advertiser takes the risk of a non-action advert, while still providing listing for your business. Affiliate profit centre like Commission Junction and Nerverblue operate with this model. An example of a variant of CPA is **Cost Per Lead (CPL)** which is based on the user completing an action that leads to you capturing a lead for your business.

Cost Per Mille (CPM)

This form of advertising is also called "Cost Per Thousand impressions (CPT), and it is a setup that exits to allow your business to pay the advertiser, when your listing has been seen by a number of people usually a thousand. It is similar to your typical newspaper ad As you are only paying to be seen. There is no additional requirement for the viewers to take action before the advertiser gets paid.

Cost Per Visitor /View (CPV)

With this form of advertising, you pay for each unique visitor brought to your online business as a result of placing the ad. CPV differs from CPC, in that with CPC each click is paid for whether the user makes it to the targeted site or not. Unlike CPV which counts only when the potential customer visits your site.

When you use the advertising methods discussed so far, always remember the aim which is to make money. Therefore, it is worth noting, that if you implement the paid advertising model, you should put together a method, of measuring the return you get for your business, compared to the cost of acquiring the customer. One will normally do this by calculating the total cost of your ad campaign and divide that by the number of sales received from it, which should give you an indication of its profitability.

If it appears unprofitable, quit running that campaign and try and analyze why. If it's unprofitable due to fundamental issues with the form of advertising implemented, then use a more suitable one. If you find out the lack of response from your market, is due your message, then address that shortfall by going back to the basics of understanding your customer. But whatever you do measure everything and make sure there justify your running them.

Before we carry on with the discussions on other types of advertising, it is worth discussing how we would go about using PPC and CPM which Google offers as advertising options for our online beauty business for example.

The first step in the process, would be to review the keywords found during the keyword research phase, carried out in chapter 3. When doing this you are looking to select keywords that will target your potential customers, and has reasonable estimates of cost per click .

For instance if you were looking to start your online beauty business by providing skin care products, then you will be looking to select keywords associated with skin care from the list of keywords saved during the keyword research. You are best to start with a few keywords about skincare, and make changes as required. The aim here is to have the right keywords to trigger the right people interested in what you have to offer. As an example, I have chosen the following keywords as ones you could use for the Google Adword campaign for your skin care products/services:
"skincare", "skin care products", "skin for men", "skin and beauty", "skin & beauty", "skin tips", "tips for skin",

"skin makeup", "makeup for skin", "glowing skin", "natural skin care".

Picking the right keywords are like picking highly effective and profitable sales people. The difference is that keywords work night and day to bring in potential customers. There reach millions doing what there do best, and the result is a highly sort after cash machine system.

Beyond PPC, Google Adwords also offers CPM advertising model, however you ad will be excluded from Google search and partners searches, and will only be displayed with Google partners, that is other sites that allow for Google Ads to be displayed on their sites. The key to setting up a successful campaign, is to start from the knowledge garnered from your research and focus on using targeted keywords. In addition, using targeted headlines to create interest with a brief description to get interested prospects to click your ads are crucial.

Even more crucial is testing and monitoring the ads placed, and refining and adjusting ads at reasonable intervals. To do this you use two important metric. One of these metric is referred to as the "impression", which provides data on the number of times your ad is displayed in front of prospective customers. The other important metric captures the prospects clicks on the ad and that action is referred to as a "click through" with the metric referred to as click through rate (CTR) which measure the percentage of clicks on your ads over the impression for your ads. Both metrics are important in measuring the effectiveness of the ad placed

Your goal is to improve the CTR which ultimately determines the performance of your ads and also the frequency for which your ad is shown i.e. its impressions. If your ads is based on CPC a comparatively low CTR ad over the course of time will reduce its quality, in the eyes of the advertiser, and they will choose to display ads with higher CTR to generate more income at the expense of yours. Also a higher CTR will help reduce your bidding cost of the clicks on your ads.

Thus, there may be a number of parameters to adjust within your ads, to improve CTR. As an example you may look at ways to improve some aspect of the body of the ads after a week, and probably some aspect of the headline after a month. The CTR data for the keywords used are usually provided by the advertiser. Think of the process as the top athletes do, when approach their sports. They are constantly striving to become the best, no reason why this can't be you. Uniquely this sets you apart from the masses, and really makes you feel special.

Beyond CTR you want to also measure the conversion rate performance of the traffic coming into your site. You can do this, through the use of tracking software that specifically monitors your sites and determines what click converts to sales. Obviously it goes without saying that you want to repeat those elements of your advertising, that results in sales or some sort of desired outcome. This is to allow for the improvement of the overall performance of your advertising and marketing efforts. In order to attain your goals of making money from your online business. I will discuss how you go about tracking your ads in chapter 6.

One of the challenges you may encounter when looking to advertise online, is choosing from the various advertising models discussed so far. Advertising online is only beginning to enter its maturity phase, and as such some things are still up in the air. In addition the model you use will depend on the niche you choose and the type of offer you intend to promote.

Broadly speaking, the way to go if you are starting online, would be to use the CPC model initially. The reason for this, is because your interest and the interest of the advertising companies are some worth intertwined, as they make money from clicks to your ads, and so will look to place your ad in a favorable location to increase exposure, and test that it is a money making ad for them.

Hence, you can run the CPC ad as test ads, and build your knowledge on the cost and performance of an optimal ad within the niche of your choice. Once you have built that knowledge, you could gradually look to move some ads to the CPM model, and verify that you are getting similar CTR and compare the cost. You may find that the CPM model works out cheaper once you understand the behavior of prospects within the niche. I have chosen not to mention CPA as an option, for now, as it requires you to have a few thousand dollars in ad budget for most of the CPA networks to consider your campaign.

Now that you understand how you may be charged for placing ads, you need to now also understand the various mechanisms for which advertising is made available to your online business.

Types Of Advertising

It is virtually impossible to have an exhaustive list of the various types of advertising available online, which is due in part to the innovative and dynamic nature of the field online. However I have outlined some of the matured types of advertising you will come across when advertising your business online.

Banner Advertising

Banner advertising is the process of using embedded graphics with text ads to entice viewers to click on ad. It is one of the oldest types of advertising done online. The banner itself is usually shaped as a bar or button containing text on a graphics background, designed to attract the viewer attention with the ultimate aim of inducing them to click on the banner. Once viewers click on the ad, they are taken directly to your website where they can then explore your offerings.

It must be said that the popularity of the banner ad online is waning, as viewers feel it distracts them from their goal of information seeking. As such there are a number of browsers and add-on that prevents the display of banner ads

Text Advertising

Similar to banner ad in that it is placed to induced action from the viewer. Text ads are fast becoming the dominant form of online advertising today, as there do not appear as distracting to the viewer as banner ads are. Google Adword makes use of text ad in its search marketing provision, where the ads are displayed as sponsored ads, or in some instance displayed within a the websites of display partners that fit within the context of the ads. A sort of contextualized framework, known as contextual advertising. The key to the ads is the headline and supporting text with a link to your site.

Interstitials Advertising

Interstitial ads are simply ads that are displayed in transition between two web pages on a site. As an example, you click on a link on a page let say the page in question is the home page, the link you clicked on, is meant to take you to the blog page. However, instead of taking you to the blog page, you arrive at an intermediate page containing a sales pitch with a link to the blog page. That sales pitched intermediate page forms the concept of this ad type. The advertising concept is becoming popular as it provides a wider scope for advertiser to sell products.

Pop-Up Advertising

If you have had any dealing online, you would have come across Pop up ads. This is basically another way of advertising your business online. However I am sure your experience are like most, in that you probably found them very annoying. If used properly and well targeted, there may bring in some traffic. But its image online is so poor that most people end up placing pop blocker, preventing the display of pop-up ads. Hence the irony.

Floating Advertising

Floating ads as the name alludes to, are ads that float on the web page. It is effectively an improvement on pop up ads and appears on a web page when a viewer first loads the page. The ads typically last for a few seconds and are usually animated and thus grab the attention of the viewer and get them to take action by clicking on the ads.

Opt-In Mailing/Email Marketing

There are a number of companies, know as email brokers, that specialize in collecting email addresses of people, grouped into a number of niches, for whom your products or services, may be of interest. They usually build these lists through a process called opt-in, which is when a person indicates by providing their name and email address, an interest in a specific offering.

It should not be confused with spam which is as a result of unwanted mails sent to recipients. With this ad form, if done properly, the prospect would have been qualified and would have given permission by providing their email to be contacted.

However there are unscrupulous mailing list brokers out there who do not care a hoot about acting ethically. As such, care should be taken when looking to use this form of advert as an alternative to reaching prospective customers.

In the long run, building your own mailing list is a better strategy, as you are able to guarantee the prospects are genuine. In addition, since you are building the list, the chances of you developing and establishing a relationship with them, would have being carried out, before selling to them. Look to use email programs called auto-responders, to automate and manage your correspondence with your mailing list, as there enable you to organize and sequence your mail to your prospective customers. The two popular ones at the time of writing are Getresponse and Aweber

Search Engine Optimization (SEO)

If you go by most of the statistics online regarding traffic, it is said that the search engines has the most traffic. And as such if one is able to tap into this traffic source, then your business should gain from the millions of traffic gravitating to the search engine daily. This search engine phenomena has lead to the birth of a field referred to as SEO

SEO is not strictly advertising, rather it is a marketing strategy that fits into the search engine marketing approach. However, I have included it under this section to discuss the paid version of SEO as it fits well within the paid advertising theme.

SEO is effectively the process of improving the amount of traffic you get to your website from various search engines. The strategy involves working with a SEO specialist to optimize your site and align your site to what the search engines are looking for.

Whatever you do, avoid the "Black Hat SEO techniques, which are attempts in fooling search engines to improve the ranking of your site on their database, and as such gain traffic to your website. In the long run this strategy will fail your business, and could get your site banned. In addition, the search engine providers, change their algorithm frequently and usually make them void.

In fact because search engines are not paid for the traffic they send to your website, they do not feel compelled in keeping the search algorithm static, and are constantly changing algorithms in an effort to improve the service offered to people using their search engine. This is what bedevils the field of SEO, as there are no guarantees that what works today will work tomorrow.

However, there are good aspects of SEO which one can implement irrespective of the search engine. This approach will also establish your presence online and equate to more traffic over time.

Unpaid Advertising

This takes time and effort to setup, in some instances, an element of technical skill is needed to implement the steps required. However, there are valuable methods for promoting your business online and does not involve you paying for the privilege.

Link Exchanges

This is when you apply a strategy of asking for your website address to be placed as a link on someone else's website, and at the same token you place their website address, as a link on your website. It is important to stress that for this strategy to be successful, you will need to only exchange links with businesses that are complementary to your business. The reason for this, is broadly due to the fact that your aim is to attract qualified prospects from other websites, to yours. And conversely you are doing the same for your link partners. As such we have a symbiotic relationship between interrelated online businesses.

The way to apply this strategy is to do a search for complementary website within your niche, go through the websites and assess which one is beneficial for your business to link with it. Once you are happy that the site is of value, find out what the email address of the owner of the site is. If there is no email on the site, you can look to use the "who is" service located here -> http://www.whois.net/ to lookup the owner of the website. Once you have located an email address for the website, send a polite mail to the webmaster (owner of the website), telling them why you feel there is mutual benefit in a link exchange with your website.

In addition to finding website to link to manually, you can also use an automated system to do the initial legwork of getting related websites for you. You can then proceed to selectively choose which site to link with. Look to have a page that you can organize as a useful resource for your viewers, with links to your link partners.

The key to maintaining an effective link exchange strategy is to have quality content on your website, keeping it fresh and new. The more you build quality links to your site the more presence you have online, and the more traffic gets routed to your online business. The other types of promotions discussed next, are simply more ways of providing links to your website.

Article Marketing

Article marketing as the name alludes to, is the art of using articles to promote your business online. It requires time and effort, and an enjoyment for what you are writing about, to continuously write articles. It is a way of creating links from high traffic source, through your published articles to your online business.

The good thing about article writing is that, the more you are able to write quality articles, the more your credibility rises online. The way it works is you write and submit your article to a dedicated article sites like Ezinearticles or Goarticles, and as part of the article you add a link to your website.

Since the article sites get lots of traffic it holds that some of those traffic should eventual land on your website. At the beginning of your online business, you may have to add article writing as part of your task for marketing your business and building your business online. As your business grows, you could look to outsource the writing of articles to other experts within your niche.

Blogs And Forum Marketing

Blogs and forum marketing are similar to article marketing, in that the concept is about writing and putting a link to your website. You can create and maintain a blog page on your website, writing on topics of interest within your niche. What could be even better, is if viewers begin to comment on them, thereby creating more interesting content on your site. In addition, you could make contributions to important blogs in your niche, putting your website address as a link on the blog entries you create. The information you provide on your blog needs to be informative and of use to your readers and you have to maintain a level of consistency with your blog updates. What this means, is updating your blog once a day, once a week, etc, so your users anticipate and come back for fresh quality content.

A similar approach could be carried out on forums, as forums are where people with problems requiring solutions converge. You could look to answer some of their questions and provide a link to your site. You could also start your own forum, and allow people to comment, creating great content on your site and a sort of consumer intelligence database, that you can then use to improve your business.

Remember as part of your niche research you investigated some top ranked forums, and made your decision to go with the niche based in part on what you found out from these forums. Thus you should start your forum marketing campaign, by going back to these forums and helping out your niche. I have so far mentioned the word forum marketing which could be misleading. In reality most forums will not let you make any form of blatant marketing like placing of links within the content of your post. What they do offer is a signature plugging, which is seen alongside your post. Hence, you can look to place your website link within your signature.

Start initially by building relationship within the forum and get yourself known by the community. Commit to posting a few times a week to maintain a level of consistency. Make yourself the go to person for solutions to problems.

Social Media Marketing

Social media is becoming a great way to market your online business. It follows a similar format to what we have already discussed regarding blogging and posting on forums. However, what you have here is a whole new source of customers and an amazing opportunity to spread the message about your online business. Some the popular social networks includes services like Facebook, Twitter, Myspace, and Likedin.

Social media allows you to develop an identity for your online business, build its brand and build relationships with other members of the communities. With the right message, your business has the potential to go viral on social networks. Hence the need to use these sites in promoting your online business effectively.

An additional use of social media beyond social network is now seen with the concept of social bookmarking. This is when users store and manage bookmarks of websites that members of that community are able to see and use.

In a nutshell if a user visits your site and loves the content you provide, they could save the link to your site as a bookmark for others to see and go to. They serve as a mouthpiece for your business, because they are able to rate your site encourage more social bookmarks to it and increase your web presence. You could also do the same for your website and make it know on these sites. Some of the popular social bookmarking sites are Delicious and Stumbleupon.

To get your online business going, it is important to reach the critical mass required to sustain your business. No one method is enough to sustain your business online. you will need to use a combination of methods which will range from reaching out to customers, and allowing customers to reach you. There is no best combination out there and a lot will depend on the business you choose to run online. Think of the process of marketing your business as an alchemic process that requires a level of ingenuity to succeed.

However, with all the methods discussed so far, underlies and important fact. That is one based on serving your prospective customer. Thus in all you do bear them in mind. For example if you are looking to write an article or blog, review the search database to see what interest your niche, and write your articles and blog from that stand point. Give them titles that will attract your prospect to them, and deliver on the content provided. The combination will guarantee success in attracting traffic to your site.

Interestingly, comparison can be drawn between your online business and the Hollywood business. I am sure you have witnessed some of the incredible blockbuster movies, that have made millions of dollars in their opening week. And have gone on to break records.

What is even more noticeable, is how key actors and actresses, go on publicity campaigns to drum up interest for the movie at hand. The result is they become richer and more famous through success in the box office. Sometimes the average person, does not realize, this people are just like them.

Who can forget George Lucas the stars wars legend. Here is his take on the first few years of his business. "My first six years in the business were hopeless. There are a lot of times when you sit and you say "Why am I doing this? I'll never make it. It's just not going to happen. I should go out and get a real job, and try to survive."

We are mostly grateful he pressed on, look to do the same for your online business, the world need you, and you can surely make it. Get the megaphone and get going.

5 HOW TO START PRINTING MONEY BY CONVERTING TRAFFIC

In the mythical world of finance, printing money is the norm. Central banks are at it, commercial banks do the same through the creation of debt. I call all this a sort of Houdini confidence trick to wealth. The other day, I was reliably informed, that one of the central bankers will stop at nothing to encourage spending. He will even go as far as printing money, and then flying through the country dropping bundles. All this to get people spending. What a life. The closest thing you will get to achieving this feat online, is to press the right button that result in sales.

You have done all you can to get traffic and you are now ready to create your own ATM. One of your most important job as the owner of an online business, will be to convert these traffic to sales. It is quite obvious you will not be in a position to convert all the traffic that heads to your website to sales. Yet what is certain, is you will need to convert a reasonable percentage of those traffic to sales. Without this you won't be as successful as you can be. This is why this chapter focuses on the process of converting sales, in order to make you a winner.

As the owner of an online business, you need to understand that selling is not tricking anybody in buying your products or services. In fact this goes against good business practice, as you end up with no customers or referrals to grow your business. If you have carried out your initial niche research diligently, you would have come across a market with problems that requires solutions. Through your business, you are looking to provide the solutions to these problems. Simply doing this will equate to sales and profits for your business. This precludes the need to trick anybody, which you tend to see with some inexperience businesses online.

The Steps In Converting Traffic To Sales

To begin selling your product to anyone online, you have to make sure you have clearly defined why the person should buy the product or services that you offer. The individual has the choice of buying from you, buying from someone else i.e. competitors or not buying at all. So it is essential you have the required answers covered.

Once you have that nailed, you need to plan the sales process from getting traffic to sales. Here is an outline of one method I know works, and there are variations of this method, but the bottom line is a focus of converting to sales at some point.

1. **Firstly you generate traffic:** Traffic equates to money online. You generate the traffic, through various methods e.g. using article writing, news letter, email campaign, social media (face book twitter, you tube etc) and paid ads. Make sure as best as you can, to qualify the traffic at this stage.
2. **Building relationship with your traffic**: Once you have generated traffic to your site, you will need to begin the process of building relationship with you clients through offering value. You can do this by encouraging your traffic to join your mailing list, become a member of your site etc. The aim is to build your potential customer base.
3. **Provide value:** Once they join your mail list, you should look to provide them with some form of value

to build credibility with your prospects. Value could be provided through your blogs, free items of value, competition to win prices and more. The aim is to be consistent with your offering to your prospects.

4. **They Purchase from you:** Once you have established a good relationship with your leads, you are now in a position to convert your leads to buyers, by offering them relevant product/service of value that will solve their problems.

5. Finally you repeat the process and in some instance get referral to other prospective buyers of your products and service.

The Obstacle To Making Sales Online

The process of selling should not be looked upon as easy. It is simple when you know how, but it is not easy to sell a $1 item to anyone online, without knowing how. The reasons for this are twofold:

The prospect has a natural fear of failure, especially regarding price, and it is the greatest obstacle to them making a purchasing decision online. In addition, there are other specific areas of concerns, to which you will need to address before the prospect is likely to make a purchase from your business. Here there are:

Prospective customers are usually concern about financial security, i.e. the fear that their financial data for example credit cards details may fall into the wrong hands. Perception may not match reality here. But it does not help when you have high profile cases of hacked credit cards details. These cases, increases the fear your prospect may have, and could prevent a sale online. This is why if you are selling to consumers directly, you will need to setup a secured mechanism for collecting payment. Most web host companies will provide a secure socket layer (SSL) as a means of providing a secured mechanism for payment. It is always helpful to make this explicitly known to your customers, to reduce their uncertainty and improve sales.

A related issue is one based on privacy and the misuse of personal data. The fear of misuse of personal data have being heightened by customers having being victims of spam themselves, or have heard of others being spammed. As such to improve sales, you will need to assure them that their data will be handled with the utmost care. If you have a national data protection act, then you can assure your customers that you subscribe to such act.

Beyond issues around data, you need to find a way of assuring the prospective customer, that the quality of the product and services offered match the description provided. In addition you should provide your name or business name on your site, email address, potential telephone number for which the customer can reach on incase anything goes wrong. All this builds confidence and helps with the sales process.

This is why going through the process I outlined previously helps in reducing the fear level of the prospect. By removing the feeling they may have, regarding the possibility of making a mistake, by buying what you offer. Because the process builds a level of trust between the prospect and your business.

In addition to building trust, you should also look to do whatever you can, to reduce the resistance to buying. One sure way is to increase the motives of your prospects wanting the product you offer. There are six prime motives that motivates a person to buy, and there are as follows

- Buying for love
- Buying for gain
- Buying for pride
- Buying for self-indulgence
- Buying for self-preservation.

Your job is to use these motives honestly in selling your products, and making them strong enough to reduce the fear of failure highlighted.

To add to the obstacle associated with the prospect, the second major obstacle to selling to the prospect is the fear of asking for the sale from your prospect. We somehow feel funny asking for a sale as if it is something to feel bad about. In most cases if you don't ask for the sale you will not get it, so make sure your online business has a way of asking for sale, either through newsletters, somewhere on your website etc. The fear of rejection is the Achilles heel of many would be sales. The key is to get the prospect to take action. If you feel fearful doing this, I suggest you face your fear and do it. The more you do it the less fearful you become, and the more you get to understand selling to being a number game.

This leads us to the point of trying to understand what the main elements are in selling or converting traffic. In truth the main element for selling or converting traffic is based on your psychology and thinking, and here are some characteristics, you will need to develop to successfully sell profitably online.

Required Personality Traits

- You need to have a high level of self confidence. The more you like yourself is the more you will like others and that includes your prospective customers. The more you like them is the more you are willing to help them, and consequently the more they are willing to stay with your business by buying from you. People will normally buy from only those they like, so it is worth bearing this in mind.

- You have to be enthusiastic about your business, and that enthusiasm will eventually become infectious and rub off on your clients. Selling in any business including online, is the transfer of your enthusiasm for the product or service you provide to your customer. What is interesting is your customers then become advocates for your business.

- You have to have a high level of empathy for your online customers. You must want to help them with their problems.

- You have to be intensely goal oriented.

- You have to have high level of will power and determination to succeed in selling online.

- You really have to believe in the products or services you are looking to sell online, before your customer in turn will believe in it.

- You have to be honest, and that is with yourself and your customers.

Everything mentioned so far are learnable skills. Hardly do you find anybody that start up with all of them. It a similar process to fine wine. There get natured to that point of absolute bliss. The same is likely applicable to you. All you need is a little bit of nurturing to accomplish great things.

Set Goals For Your Sales

Sales goals are of upmost importance to your online business. As such you need to measure the traffic required to get X amount of sales for your business. You may find for instance, that your business requires "a thousand traffic to make five sales". You need to know this, to be able to determine what to do to manage your online business. You also need to work out what the average lead time is from getting traffic to converting that traffic into a paying customer. This will allow for better planning of your sales. I have outlined what you need to know to guide your daily activities for your online business.

- What is your annual income goal and what is the sales volume required to hit that goal?
- How much does your business need to earn monthly to reach your annual goal?
- What is the monthly traffic and sales volume required to reach the required monthly income goal?
- How much does your business need to earn weekly to reach your monthly goal?
- What is the weekly traffic and sales volume required to reach the required monthly income goal?

- How much does your business need to earn daily to reach your weekly goal?
- What is the daily traffic and sales volume required to reach the required weekly income goal?

It is worth remembering that your online business is there to meet your financial goals discussed is chapter two. So you need to use the financial goal you defined previously, to plan your business sales. You want to define how to meet the sales goals, by the activities discussed previously for completing sales online. For example if I calculated that I need a thousand traffic daily to meet my annual sales goal, then the fundamental question would be what do I need to do, to attract a thousand traffic a day. Here is an example of how your activities can be designed to be aligned to the sales goal of attaining 1000 traffic a day.

Example of A Daily Business Activities To Target Sales

- You need 10 Link exchanges with other similar themed websites daily
- You need to write two articles and post on a number of article sites daily
- You need to write one blog entry on your blog daily
- You need to post an entry in your niche forums daily
- You need to send 10 tweets on twitter and 10 posts on facebook about your business daily.
- You need to place 10 ads on free classified ads and more.

You can see how one begins to tie in the activities we have discussed so far, with your ultimate goal of making money through your online sales. This is why it stands without mentioning that in order to be successful with your online business you have to choose the right business that you have a passion for and there is demand for it. There are so many opportunities online, that makes very possible for you.

Offline Sales

If you can, do not confine your online business to just online methods of reaching customers. Look to make use of some of the existing methods of reaching customers offline. I have listed some of them below:

Face to Face sales: it is still very much easier to sell to someone face to face than it is selling online, so if an opportunity for this exists, you should explore this with your potential clients. Things like free seminars to discuss your products and service is a good way of achieving sales for your online business.

Telesales: You can use this as a way of letting potential clients know your business exist and getting them to go to your site and explore your offerings.

Direct mail: Direct mail is another effective way of selling your products and services offline, especially when done properly.

Use your business artifacts like the following to promote your online business:

- Letterhead
- Envelopes
- Invoices
- Sales letters

- Business cards
- Receipts
- Brochures
- Flyers
- Phone book list.

Converting your traffic to sales is the lifeblood of your business online, and should be taken seriously. The only way to improve sales just like marketing, is to measure and improve your conversion rate.

Study the traffic coming into your site , find out which of the keyword brings them in, understand how they arrive at your site, i.e. finding out the source of the traffic. Find out which of the traffic, based on keywords or source of traffic converts to the most sales. Once you know this information look to optimize your website to be better aligned to such favorable traffic.

As an example if you find out people locate your site through a number of keywords and those people convert well to sales. This is telling you something about the behavior pattern of a profitable group of customers within your niche. Therefore, what you will look to do is optimize the content(using the appropriate keywords) of your sites. Also doing the same for the technical element of your web pages by optimizing them, with the appropriate keywords, in order to better align them to the profitable traffic source.

Focus your effort on finding and nurturing profitable customers. This is a continuous effort and it is typical of most successful online business. To be successful online, you cannot afford to be lazy.

6 SLICK TECHNOLOGY BEHIND YOUR ONLINE RICHES

A big aspect of your online business is the technology that underpins the business. As stated previously you do not require in dept technical grasp to manage your online business successfully. Most elements of the technology used, are easily delegated to others. However, due to the importance of technology to your business, a clear understanding of how there are aligned in supporting your online business, is of the utmost importance in attaining excellence through your business.

If you don't believe knowing the details of any business, breeds excellence which underpins the success of your business. You should read what Andrew Carnegie, had to say about this. "And here is the prime condition of success, the great secret. Concentrate your energy, thoughts and capital exclusively upon the business in which you are engaged in. Having begun in one line, resolve to fight it out on that line; to lead in it. Adopt every improvement, have the best machinery and know the most about it." The operative word by Mr. Carnegie is for you to know the most about your business to be successful.

The best way in understanding the supporting technology of your business, is to take a bird eye view i.e. one that resonates from the customer experience and gradually works its way down to the nuts and bolts that supports the overall infrastructure. You do this by working your way from the design of your website down to the backend devices used in supporting your site.

Design Of The Website

In order to understand why the design of your website is crucial to your success online, imagine what successful businesses, like the supermarkets do offline. If you are in the U.S, you would have witnessed the dominance of Wal-Mart. The same applies to U.K residence, who are also able to attest to the success of Tesco. Why are these businesses so successful?

One of the major reason for these successes, is due in part to their understanding of their customers. This is reflected in the design or the layout of their aisle, and placement of groceries. When you walk in as a customer, you are greeted with a lovely smell, that arouses your hunger for the items on display. Incidentally items associated with kids are placed mid to bottom of the aisle, at eye levels for children to see and get parents to buy. Everything is designed and placed to induce the customer to buy as much as they can, removing any impediment to achieving this goal.

A further example can be seen with Google. Do you know why Google is one of the most popular website out there? Apart from the fact that they have designed a fit for purpose search algorithm, they are also one of the top website used, because they spend tremendous amount of time and effort getting their website designed right for their customer. Thus giving the user/customer of their website a fulfilling experience. A similar experience is seen with Apple's IPod and IPad products and the enhance enjoyable experience customers get using these products.

This is what you should look to achieve for your website. This is not to say you should spend all your time on the technology element of your business, at the expense of your content and other aspects of your business. After all anyone in business know sales and marketing are the lifeblood of any business. Yet in order to maintain and improve sales, you will need to make sure the customers arriving at your site get the required user experience to fulfill your call of action which is sales. Think of it as part of selling through providing a full service.

Imagine yourself a Hollywood director, and the website your blockbuster movie. This is what is required to create a website that holds the interest and engages with customers online. Users online are notoriously flighty and will not hesitate to leave your site in seconds of arrival. Hence what is required is for you to create a customer experience that results in sales of your product(s) or service(s).

Before beginning the process of designing your website for the experience you hope to induce within your prospective customers. You need to clearly decide the focus of the entire website. Is your website going to be information based, ecommerce based or a mixture of both. In addition, develop focused web pages which are the building block of your website.

An advice here is to refer back to your research carried out previously. Select a number of top keywords you found that were used by prospects to locate information online. Then develop WebPages per keyword, and provide the information/products that matches those keywords on each webpage. The advantage you get by doing this, is that you are more likely to design and structure your website to be better aligned to your customer needs. This will enhance their overall experience when they visit your site.

In order to fulfill the user experience so far mentioned, you should look to adopt the following goals. This will aid in your achieving your aim during the design phase of your website.

User Experience Goals

Accessibility: This is probably one of the most important goal to achieve for your website. Accessibility involves making your sites accessible to people with challenging needs. They include but are not limit to individuals that are visually impaired or blind, individuals that are deaf, individuals that are slightly impaired due to age and more.

In addition, if you are intending for your website to be properly indexed and found by the search engines. Then you will to design your site for the search engine robot. This robot trawl the web and locate the content on your site, and is both deaf and blind. Therefore, it pays your business, that you prevent inaccessibility to your website by the search robot. Since you are ultimately looking to make money online, and the prevention of your website from been found, will have a detrimental effect on achieving this goal.

Furthermore your potential customers may access your site through mobile devices, or low speed connections, which may prevent viewing by these set of customers, if your website is not optimally designed to be accessible by them.

When you are designing your website to be accessible, one of the important challenges to resolve, are image contents within your site. This are unlikely to be seen by those that are blind, and as such will need an alternative way for them to picture the image provided on your site. HTML (which is the computer language that describe WebPages) comes with a mechanism that allows you to provide an alternative text description to fully describe the image. This will allow screen reader software to describe the image to the customer. Make sure you always use the alternate text description for every image on your site.

The other key challenge as mentioned previously, is providing for individuals that have a hearing impediment. If you have a video content on your site that provides important information during the sales process for instance. You will need a way of making this information available to others unable to hear the video, or have turned the video off on their web browsers, may be due to the bandwidth required in viewing the video on online. Thus you will need to have the audio element of the video transcribed in order to provide the required information to others unable to view the video in its entirety.

The principle behind accessibility of your website is to provide alternative access for those unable to view or access your site through the standard mechanism. Designing your website to be accessible varies in complexity, depending on the content of your site and the complexity of the site. The World Wide Web Consortium (W3C) deals extensively with this issue, and can be an additional source of aid, in designing your website to be accessible http://www.w3.org/

The website must have the right content: The content will make or break your website and as such has to fulfill a number of objectives. It has to be valuable to the intended customer, it has to be interesting and engaging, and finally it has to be delivered in a format that encourages consumption of the content.

Getting the valuable content right, as discussed, is down to your understanding what your customer want, which as touched on previously you can delineate from your initial market research and continuous understanding of your customer.

To create the interest, you have to understand how people assimilate information. You need to have the right website and webpage tiles that customers will respond to. Use headlines within your content to catch attention and let your prospects know that your site is of interest and value to them. The reason why this is so effective is once again down to the flighty nature of people surfing online. Some of them may just scan your web page before making a decision to go through the content in more detail.

Hence, if your site is logically structured with catchy and appealing titles and headlines, it induces positive expectation on the viewer of the site. Thereby motivating them to spend time scouring the content on offer. Nowhere is this more important than the home page, which is in most times the first point of contact with your website. Although the importance of the home page has declined slightly. Due in part to people finding different gateways into your site, as a result of the indexing of individual webpage on search engines. It is still important you attend to the home page to create the right impression.

Beyond catching their interest, in order to get them engaged, to maintain their interest requires to provide compelling stories of interest. There should first and foremost be informative, but nonetheless delivered in format that keeps the prospects interested. The only way to keep people engaged and interested with the content you provide, is to build pictures of interest, within their mind. Make this part of the process of delivering your story to the viewers of your site.

To achieve, the points you intend to put across should be vividly described to allow the customer to see and feel what you are delivering to them. You can achieve this through writing word picture content, or images where appropriate. The aim is to create an image in the mind of your prospects, that will encourage them to take action. To encourage your customer to retain the information disseminated, it is worth considering their cognitive limitation. This is specifically relevant to short term memory. So deliver you content, in blocks that does not overrun this limitation.

To aid them visually, look to use at least a 12 point character size for the content on your website, and use the standard character set known to most, like Ariel and Times New Roman. Provide adequate spacing between group of writing content to aid assimilation by the viewer of your site. Cramming lots of information into a tight space creates a cluttering effect, and discourages your viewer from attending to the content on your site.

Look to make important information provided within your content better visible by making them bold or highlighted. Also use characters and background that gives a good contrast between the background color and the color of the character. Perfect example of background color that will aid consumption of content, is the use of a white background with black colored characters.

The website must be easy to navigate: The layout of your website must make it easy to reach relevant content.

This is most important to potential customers coming into your website for the first time. People do not have lots of patience, and very easily go elsewhere if they are unable to quickly locate what they are after.

This is why, one of the major design decision for your website, is how you intend to structure the site to aid the process of locating information. The best way to do this, is to think as the customer would. What would be their expectation on visiting your site? How would they expect your website to be structured? What are the most important information likely to be required by potential customers, and more. Once you have answers these questions, you can then proceed.

Look to structure and place important and most demanding information where there can be easily located. Evidence shows that important information should be placed at center top of the webpage, and then move to the top left of the page, and carry on to the right and then continue below until you have placed the least important item at the bottom of the page. What this means, is users are able to find the important aspect on the site quickly. Also if your website is to contain many pages, a hundred pages and above, you may look to add a site map. The sitemap depicts the structure of the website and aid navigation.

The website must be effective: This means the website must be design to aid users in accomplishing the required goal. This involves getting the conceptual design of the website to a point, that it is completely effective at encouraging completion of the end goal. Make sure the elements involved in supporting your customers, aids them with the task at hand.

The website must be efficient by allowing your customers, to use the shortest steps possible in accomplishing their goals. The process of using the website to complete tasks, should be streamed line to aid them with their task.

The website must be motivating, particularly motivating enough, in making customers accomplish the call to action. The way the site is put together, must motivate the primary emotions discussed in the previous chapter, to aid the buying process.

The website must be aesthetically likeable by your customers. They must like the look and feel of the website in order to encourage them to use it.

Finally the website should be helpful, offer an overall pleasurable experience to the viewer, and must not detract from the goal of the website. It is worth noting that websites can be interactive. Think of the activities involved in a sales process. How would you sell if you were face to face with a prospect. You may get to do this, by getting them involved with the process. Look to do something similar were possible at various point on your site. And make your WebPages consistent to remove element of surprise from the process.

Beyond designing the website for human consumption, you have to be aware that websites should also be designed to function within a physical context. This in turn introduces constraint to the design of your website. The context I refer to, are the software and hardware that will run and connect to your website.

The aim is to design to satisfy the software and hardware types, that are most likely to be used in viewing your site. As of the time of writing Microsoft window is still the dominant operating system in the personal computer space. With the hardware platform mainly Intel based. However, there is an emergence of a new trend, one based on the use of handheld devices for connecting to the internet. As such, your website design will need to factor this evolving trend, in order that you give your business a chance to be connected by people with these devices.

Broadly speaking a website that is better designed, with the right content for the customer, will have a competitive edge in any niche. Think big about your business, and do the same for your website. There is no need solely designing your website for today, think of how your website is likely to evolved in six months time and design for that as well. I prefer to view this as being innovative and improving the niche for the better.

As I have stated before, you do not need to design the website yourself. You can get people with experience to help with this. Or you can chose to use standard website templates that are provided by hosting companies. Nevertheless, you are now in a position, to engage properly with specialist you may intend to bring in, to develop your site. By working closely with them, you can better produce the vision you have of your site. If you choose to go the standard templates route, you can also make an informed decision on the best template for your website.

HTML And HTML Tools To Implement Your Website

Once you have decided on the design element of the website, the next port of call, is how you bring the design to life. The substantiation of the design is achieved by a markup-language, known as Hyper Text Markup Language (HTML). It is worth mentioning that some of the functions required for your website may rely on other computer programming languages like PHP, Perl, Javascript and more. But we shall only stick with HTML from a generic standpoint.

HTML instruct how the content should be interpreted and displayed by the web browser. You can think of HTML as a publishing mechanism of documents online in the form of WebPages. It achieves the description of how content should be displayed through the use of markup tags. Tags are < HTML markups within angular brackets>. Most tags will begin with an opening tag and end with a closing tag, with the content to be formatted located between both tags.

As an example to define the first header within HTML you will have the following entry:

<h1>This is the first header</h1>

The example given above is also referred to as a HTML element. The opening tag is the first tag without the /, and closing tag is the one with the /. In between both tags is the text which will be displayed as a header by the browser. Some of the popular opening and close tags are shown in the next table

Opening Tag	Closing Tag	Description
<!DOCTYPE>		Defines the version of markup language used in writing the webpage
<html>	</html>	Defines the Webpage
<head>	</head>	Defines the head which holds description of the webpage
<meta>		Descript the webpage and its content.
<title>	</title>	Describes the title of the webpage
<body>	</body>	Defines the body of the content visible to the viewer of the webpage
<h1>,<h2>,<h3>, <h4>, <h5>, <h6>	</h1>,</h2>,</h3>, </h4>, </h5>, </h6>	Describes the six header levels available in html
<p>	</p>	Describes a paragraph
<a href="www.link.com">	</a>	Describes a web link on the webpage
<table>	</table>	Describe a table
 		Defines a line break
<script>	</script>	Used to extend the webpage functionality by reference other compute program within the web pate
<div>	</div>	Define sections within the webpage

As you can see, the tags are used to format and describe the content. In addition to tags, we also have an attribute referred to as style, which you can use within most html tags, to define the look and feel of the webpage.

The introduction of a new version of HTML, version 4 to be precise, eliminates the need for including style attributes alongside contents within the html document. It achieves this by providing a mechanism for separating the style attributes/values. The separation is achieved, by defining them in a separate document called Cascading Style Sheets (CSS). This document is subsequently used by the browser to interpret the required style of the content.

It is able to do this through the <link> tag, which references the CSS document. The <link> tag is defined within the <head> tag of all the WebPages of the website, to give the site a consistent look and feel. If you want a specific style for a webpage, you can use the <style> tag to reference the CSS document, which will only format that webpage with the CSS definitions.

Finally if you are looking to format a specific element within the page, you can still use "style" attribute within a html tag associated with the content. You will need to provide the "style" attribute, with the relevant CSS values to format the content. The requirement for doing this should be few and far between if you have taken the CSS route of decoupling the styles from the content document.

There are also various HTML edit and publishing tools that allow you to develop WebPages, without the need to understand the underlining HTML. Some of these tools are Dreamweaver, NVU and Microsoft FrontPage.

Choosing Your Hosting Company

You have your website designed and implemented with HTML. In order to make it public online, you will require a mechanism for achieving this. The mechanism that allows your website to be viewed by your customer, requires a computer that is publicly connected to the internet. Most typical business will not have the time nor resource, to run a computer or server of this nature. Hence, the need to find businesses referred to as hosting companies, that offer this service.

The choices on offer for a hosting package, varies from shared server service to dedicated servers. Further choice is to be made on storage capacity, as there are various sizes of disks on offer. Add to that the different ranges of bandwidth which will be used for transferring content to and fro, and for traffic coming into your sites, and you could get yourself into a tailspin.

To avoid confusion, you need to understand the factors consider when making a choice on hosting companies. Some of the factors to consider, are performance, capacity and reliability/recoverability.

Performance and Capacity: There are a number of backend elements that affects the performance and the capacity of your website. This is apart from what and how you may have designed and implemented your website, which also matters.

Regarding performance, the bandwidths, which are the connections available for you to download and uploads files to and from your host sever may have an in pact on the performance of the service. Since traffic also connect to your server using this link, the speed and the capacity is also impacted.

In addition, there are also internal bandwidth within the server, that affects the performance of internal communication within the server. This in turn may have potential implications on your website. The speed of the disk, CPU, memory and whether it has cache will have a bearing on the performance of your site. This is apart from other aspect of the operating system used by the server, and the performance tuning activities that may or may not have been carried out by the hosting company. Which may also have an impact on the performance of your site.

Other aspect of capacity limitation, is centered round the disk. As the disk size will have a bearing, on how much data you hold on it. This may not matter much to and information site using mainly character content. But to an ecommerce site with images of products, it may become an issue. The bandwidth of the server, will have an impact on how much activity you are able to run concurrently, on the server. This may translate to an impact on the number of concurrent traffic, you are able to run at any given moment on your site.

Reliability/recoverability: The uptime is the amount of time a system is up. Or from your point of view the amount of time you web service is up during the course of the year. The server, and the connection to it will have a bearing on this figure and will ultimately determine how reliable your website is perceived by potential customers.

On the other hand, recoverability is how if act all you are able to, recover your website from a problem. This obviously is a big part of your business. It matters just like reliability, that your service is not out for an extended period. As it will affect business.

There are a number of measures that the hosting company is able to take, in order to reduce the risk to your business from the risk factors mentioned so far. In terms of reliability, running your website on a clustered resource will help reduce the risk of downtime to your service. In addition, if the clustered servers are in different location, it will further improve the reliability of your service. To add to this, offering some sort of resilience on the disk through Raid 1, 10, 5 , 6 will help with added protection over your business data, and help in ensuring that service continues if one disk fails.

With regards to recoverability, there are a number of measure mainly to do with backups, they can take, that will keep copies of your business data safe for recovery if and when required.

Before choosing a hosting company and the package on offer, carryout due diligence on the overall service offered. Understand the sort of requirements of your website in order to make the right choice. Check what others think of their hosting service. Also bear in mind some of the factors mentioned so far when looking for the right hosting company for your business. A bit of work before hand saves on any potential heartache.

Tools to Track Traffic and measure performance of the business.

You are at a point where you have completed your site, found a hosting company, and began your marketing and sales campaign. However, as discussed in the previous chapter, you will require a means of tracking and improving your business based on the information gathered.

Google analytic and Yahoo analytic are both free tools that will track the source of your traffic, and provide data on the "impression"(the amount of time the your website appear on search) and CTR (the percentage of clicks to your sire over impression) metrics. All you need to do in the case of Google is open a free account, and copy the html code to your website, making sure your website is already submitted and indexed by Google.

For yahoo, you will need to open a Yahoo advertising or Yahoo Small Business account, also making sure your site is already submitted and indexed by Yahoo. Both search engine providers, offer tools that provides you with the ability to verify that your website is indexed by them. Google Webmaster tool have other tools that are complementary to their analytics which you can further use in understanding traffic coming into you site.

However, just understanding where traffic are coming from and what keywords brings them in is not enough. You need to also understand the behavior of your potential customers once they arrive on your site. In order to improved or optimize your site to their requirements.

Some hosting companies, offer as part of their package, tracking programs that fulfill this objective. Hence, you may be best served putting this down as part of your requirement when looking for a hosting package. In addition there are other free and paid software that are geared to tracking clicking activities on your site. These tools can also provide the additional insight you are after. Some of the available free software are as good as the paid once, and a simple search on one of the search engines, should throw up a number of tools you could explore.

Getting informed on the nuts and bolts supporting your online business enables you to make informed decision that benefits your business. You now understand what you are able to take on, and what you may need to delegate to others. In general, the more you know about your business, the more chances you have of making it a success.

When one refers to making your business a success, it is always worth seeing what other think of this. Tim Blixseth a successful entrepreneur once said "The turning point, I think, was when I really realized that you can do it yourself. That you have to believe in you because sometimes that's the only person that does believe in your success but you."

This is what this chapter is really about, to show you can be the master of the details and become the frontrunner in the eyes of your customers. You can make a difference with your business in spite what others may think.

7 BEGIN TO UNDERSTAND HOW TO PROTECT YOUR WEALTH

If you feel marketing and selling may not be for you, or you feel you would like a form of passive income or want to have a better understanding of how to manage your finances that you will hopefully have accrued from your other online business, then learning how to do this in the stock market or any financial market, may be crucial to your diversification strategy. Here are some of the reasons why you will find the financial markets interesting. I have chosen to outline them in a question and answer format to aid in understanding.

Why The Financial Market Business?

Because there are numerous opportunities available in making money in the financial market. Below are some of the benefits of the financial market.

- You can make money under any economic conditions recession or expanding economy.
- You can make money when asset prices go up, or even when there go down.
- You can make money in any financial market e.g. stock market, currency market, commodity market and bonds market.
- You can be in profits within weeks.
- You can run the business from home.
- In some cases you can make money tax free.
- It is one the few businesses where the common man can turn a small amount to a fortune.

- You can get a rewarding intellectual pursuit from the business.
- Very minimal start up capital is required.
- You don't need Staff.
- It is a well established business with a proven track record.
- You don't need to market or sell any product or services.

Why do majority of the people fail in this business and any other business?

- They don't have a plan.
- They don't follow a plan.
- They are not focused.
- They are not disciplined.
- They are not willing to work at it.
- They easily give up.
- They don't believe in themselves.
- They, in some perverse way, want to lose.

Why do a few succeed in this business?

- They have self belief.
- They invest in themselves.
- They have a plan and they follow it.
- They are patient and disciplined.
- They are focused on being the best at trading and investing.
- They want to win.

- They accept complete responsibility of outcomes.
- They are continuously learning.

Who are the Financial Market Participants?

In order to participate effectively in the financial markets, we need to understand the types of participants involved in the market. They are broadly three types of participants in the market, which are based on how long participants typically hold on to an asset.

Short term market participants

They generally own assets from a few seconds to a day. They are private day traders, market maker or scalpers, proprietary or institutional traders, short term arbitrageurs, information or events traders, outright gamblers etc. They are characterized by fast acting and high turnover of assets. The advantages of this type of market participation, is that you get quick feedback from the market, and in most cases capital are not tied for a long period, which means there can be used in other market opportunities. In addition, you are not faced with overnight risk, as the transactions are generally closed before the end of the trading day.

The disadvantages are the amount of trading commission generated by this type of activity, the risk of getting sucked in by the market into always doing something, which may lead to overtrading, and in most instances not allowing for enough time to making positive returns on market positions if strategy is based on trade price direction.

The ideal strategy for this time range are those that have a non-directional slant, i.e. strategies that make money based on receiving spreads, like market markers, or one that corrects short-term price relationship discrepancies between related securities i.e. arbitrageurs strategies.

Medium Term market participants

These are market participants that general own assets from between a day to a year. They are short term swing momentum traders, position traders, spread traders, growth investors etc. They are characterized by medium to slow acting and medium to slow turnover of assets. The advantages of this type of market participation, is that you give the trades enough time to confirm your opinions. The commission fees are a lot less than frequent shorter term trades. The disadvantages are the overnight risk inherent in holding these types of positions, and the larger risk incurred in holding positions for longer time period.

Long Term market participants

These are market participants that general own assets for more than a year. There are interested in the value appreciation and income generated from assets. They are value investors, income seeking investors, etc. They are characterized by slow acting and low turnover of assets. The advantages and disadvantages are similar to those of the medium term participants.

As a market participant, you will be operating within a specific type time frame, or may prefer to sit within a hybrid position, in order to take advantage of certain market time frame characteristics. You also will be using one or more strategies to approach the market.

However, the key to all this is to develop a strategy with an EDGE based on your circumstance, temperament, experience and the appropriate financial vehicle.

What Exactly Is The Financial Market?

The financial market is a market that allows participants to lay claim on real assets, with the intentions of profiting from their claims on these assets. A transaction is completed when you have a buyer and a seller agree on a price to purchase the financial asset or security.

The claims made could be based purely on anticipation of the real assets appreciating in value which should translate into price appreciation in the financial market (all things being equal) or the claim could be made solely on the basis of yield/income generated by the real asset. This again should result in income paid to holders of these assets.

There are two groups of financial assets and there are as follows:

- Fixed Income Market

- Capital / Non Fixed Income Market

Fixed Income Market

This market consists of assets that are in the form of loans issued by governments, banks and other big companies looking to raise capital from the market. The loans are debts owed by the institution issuing them, to the market participants who provide the capital required. The loans are issued in a form of an "I Owe You Note "indicating the amount required. In return the holders of the notes are rewarded with interest paid on the capital provided, hence the term fixed income.

Fixed income market is further divided into money market and long term bonds assets. Money market assets are effectively short term with duration of usually under a year.

While the bonds market on the other hands are longer term loans made to the institutions by the market participants. In both instances the capital provided by the market is guaranteed by the institutions that receive them.

Capital / Non Fixed Income Market

This market consists of financial assets that do not guarantee a fixed income during their duration. The markets involved in the buying and selling of these assets are the equity/ stock market, and the derivative markets. The derivative market further consists of future and option contracts used to lay claims on assets like commodities, currencies and other exotic assets.

At this point, it would be right to assume that most people may not know the intricacies of the stock market, but intuitively know it is a market for buying and selling various companies shares. The shares sold, being a claim to a part of the company underlying assets.

However the derivative markets may not be as well known, and will be explained in the following subsection:

Derivative Market

The derivative markets, are markets that track the price of underlying assets and increases or decreases in value based on the movement of price of the underlying assets. In other words its value is derived directly from the price fluctuations of the market which it tracks. The main difference between the derivative markets and the equity market, is unlike the equity market where you invest and effectively part own the company, with derivatives, their main purpose is not to invest, but to enable the transfer of risks from the real economy (which consists of producers, users, distributors and manufacturer of real assets) to the financial market.

The reason the derivative market exist in the first place, is because businesses mainly want to know how much they will pay for a commodity or how much there will get from selling a commodity, in order to be able to plan and manage their businesses. However the assets, to which they deal with mainly commodities and currencies, tend to fluctuate in price, hence their difficulty in planning and managing their businesses, and the need in transferring the risk to a third party.

Thus, the transfer of risk to the derivative market achieves the transfer of the "price risk" previously grappled by businesses, to the derivative market. Since the price of these assets can go up and come down representing the "price risk", market participants are able to make money when the prices goes up and when there also go down depending on their position in the market.

In a nutshell the financial market provides an additional opportunity to diversify your online business. In addition, even if you are not looking to manage your investments yourself, you should always remember you are fully responsible for your own finances, and as such having the skills to manage those delegated in managing your portfolio is essential in today's climate of uncertainty. So learning the skills could be seen as a wise investment.

8 CONCLUSION

To begin anything in life, you should look to start by developing yourself. But do not wait to complete this task before going for your dreams. An attitude like that of Mary Kay Ash, founder of Mary Kay Cosmetics will surely take you places. Here is her views simply put. "When you reach an obstacle, turn it into an opportunity. You have the choice. You can overcome and be a winner, or you can allow it to overcome you and be a loser. The choice is yours and yours alone. Refuse to throw in the towel. Go that extra mile that failures refuse to travel. It is far better to be exhausted from success than to be rested from failure.".

The best thing you can do for yourself is to keep developing your mind and learning to think for yourself. Try not to limit your potential in anyway, as what you are able to achieve with focus, persistence and determination is immense. Take reference from people like Colonel Sanders founder of KFC. He knew he wanted to amount to something as describe by this quote "I made a resolve then that I was going to amount to something if I could. And no hours, nor amount of labor, nor amount of money would deter me from giving the best that there was in me. And I have done that ever since, and I win by it. I know".

The one thing that befalls people is the act of thinking incorrectly. Try and think differently from the masses and you will get a different result. Most people think solely about helping themselves, without understanding, that to help yourself you have to help others. To help others you have to be of value. To be of value you have to develop your thoughts and thinking process. To develop your thoughts and thinking process, you have to develop yourself as an asset. The process of getting rich is simply a series of value exchanges. Thus aligning your thoughts along this, will bode well with the process of starting and running a successful online business. Try to always keep in mind the rewards to be had, by taking action.

In conclusion, I hope this book has been able to serve you as a simple guide in getting you started with your online business. The biggest contribution of this book is not necessarily in the details provided, but the principles provided, which will always exist irrespective of the technology used in running your business.

Businesses are based on relationships, and that includes those online. Take the simple principles offered in the book, and use them as an aid in your journey to developing a successful online business. I know you can do it, believe in yourself and give yourself a chance. So many others have taken the path before you, and the reward that was had was beyond their wildest dreams when they started. You I am sure, will be saying the same, in the not too distant future. Good luck in becoming **Rich**.

APPENDIX

A.1 Screen Capture of the top three sites for "Beauty tips" Niche on Google Search.

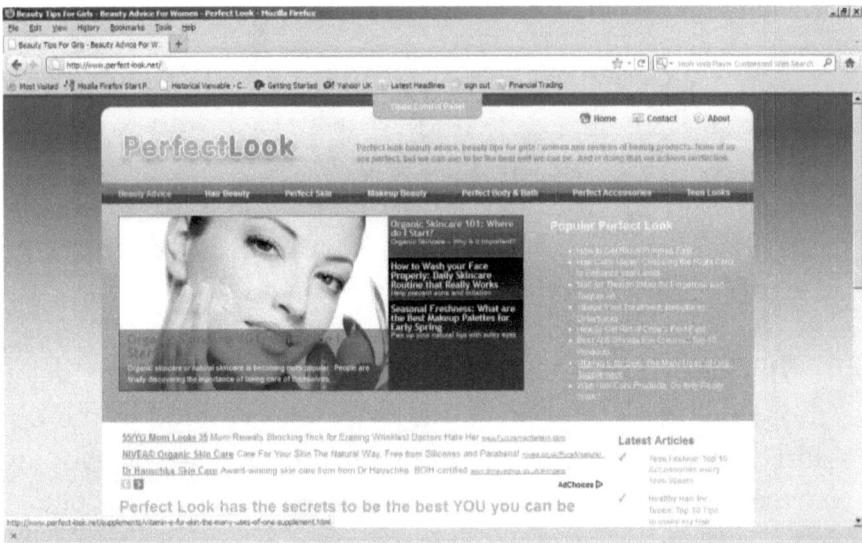

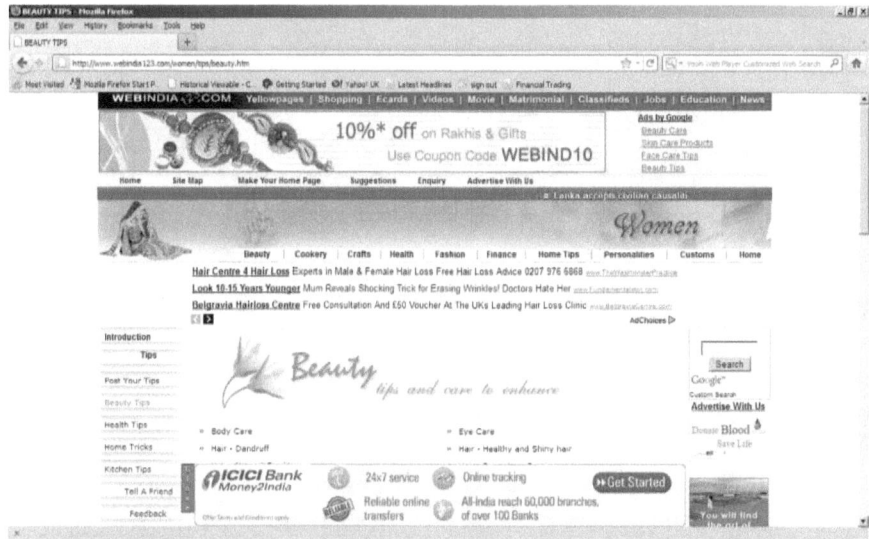

A.2 The Keywords found for the "Perfect Look" website using Google Keyword Tools
http://www.perfect-look.net/

Keyword	Global Monthly Searches	Approximate CPC (£)
hairstyles for	16600000	0.36
hairstyles hairstyles	16600000	0.37
the hairstyles	16600000	0.36
hairstyles with	16600000	0.33
a makeup	16600000	0.67
hairstyles for hair	16600000	0.33
hair hairstyles	16600000	0.36
hairstyle for	13600000	0.32
hairstyles styles	13600000	0.36
hairstyle styles	9140000	0.33
of acne	7480000	1.42
the acne	7480000	1.33
acne	7480000	1.41
cuts hair styles	7480000	0.34

hair styles cuts	7480000	0.36
haircuts and hair styles	7480000	0.32
in style hairstyles	6120000	0.37
hairstyles in style	6120000	0.37
style hairstyles	6120000	0.35
hair styles in style	6120000	0.39
style hair styles	6120000	0.37
in style hair styles	6120000	0.38
shampoo with	5000000	0.61
shampoo and	5000000	0.58
hair for short hair	4090000	0.32
for pimples	4090000	1.08
lips lip	3350000	0.5
creams for	3350000	0.86
shampoos	3350000	0.63
pimples or acne	2740000	1.2
pimples and acne	2740000	1.1
pimples acne	2740000	1.22
acne or pimples	2740000	1.11
acne and pimples	2740000	1.1
acne pimples	2740000	1.14
for scars	2740000	1.34
hair coloring	2240000	0.61
hairstyles for short	2240000	0.32
hairstyles short hairstyles	2240000	0.34
hairstyles short hair	2240000	0.34
hairstyles for short hair	2240000	0.32
short styles	1830000	0.32
hair styles for short	1830000	0.32
short hair styles for	1830000	0.34
short short hair styles	1830000	0.32
short hair styles for short hair	1830000	0.32

short hair styles short hair styles	1830000	0.31
hair styles for short hair	1830000	0.34
hair styles short hair	1830000	0.33
hair styles short	1830000	0.32
colors for hair	1830000	0.61
short hair styles cuts	1830000	0.34
hair color colors	1830000	0.64
hair for curly hair	1500000	0.64
pimple pimple	1500000	0.78
by hair products	1500000	0.77
it hair products	1500000	0.81
hair products hair products	1500000	0.81
fingernails toenails	1220000	0.38
style short hair styles	1220000	0.36
short hair styles haircuts	1000000	0.31
the wrinkle	1000000	1.24
the in hairstyles for 2010	1000000	0.39
hairstyles 2010 hairstyles 2010	1000000	0.39
the hairstyles of 2010	1000000	0.37
in hairstyles for 2010	1000000	0.41
in hairstyles 2010	1000000	0.4
hairstyles in 2010	1000000	0.4
2010 in hairstyles	1000000	0.41
hairstyles 2010	1000000	0.38
long long hair styles	1000000	0.48
hair styles in 2010	1000000	0.41
in hair styles 2010	1000000	0.42
hair styles 2010	1000000	0.39
hair styles 2010 hair styles 2010	1000000	0.4

hair styles of 2010	1000000	0.41
hair styles for 2010	1000000	0.41
2010 hair styles	1000000	0.41
hair 2010 styles	1000000	0.41
home remedy treatments	823000	1.04
nailart	823000	0.47
hairstyles for medium	823000	0.53
hairstyles with medium hair	823000	0.58
the hairstyle for 2010	823000	0.34
hairstyle of 2010	823000	0.34
haircut styles short	823000	0.3
haircut styles for short hair	823000	0.28
haircut styles short hair	823000	0.27
medium styles	673000	0.52
hair styles for medium	673000	0.53
hair styles with medium hair	673000	0.57
medium hair hair styles	673000	0.53
oil for the hair	673000	0.59
hair for oil	673000	0.59
haircuts 2010 haircuts 2010	673000	0.35
long hairstyles cuts	673000	0.47
hair styles cuts 2010	673000	0.39
nail by design	673000	0.42
design a nail	673000	0.4
a design nail	673000	0.41

A.3 The Keywords found for the "The BeautyTip.com" website using
Google Keyword Tools
http://www.thebeautytip.com/index.htm

Keyword	Global Monthly Searches	Approximate CPC (£)
hairstyles for hair	16600000	0.33
hair hairstyles	16600000	0.36
hairstyle for	13600000	0.32
hairstyles styles	13600000	0.36
hairstyle styles	9140000	0.33
in style hairstyles	6120000	0.37
hairstyles in style	6120000	0.37
style hairstyles	6120000	0.35
hair styles in style	6120000	0.39
style hair styles	6120000	0.37
in style hair styles	6120000	0.38
hair for short hair	4090000	0.32
a cut hairstyles	3350000	0.34
hair dye	2740000	0.67
hair dye hair dye	2740000	0.62
dye for hair	2740000	0.63
dye in hair	2740000	0.65
hair coloring	2240000	0.61
hairstyles short hairstyles	2240000	0.34
short hair styles short hair styles	1830000	0.31
hair styles short hair	1830000	0.33
hair styles short	1830000	0.32
colour hair dye	1830000	0.6
short hair styles hairstyles	1830000	0.34
color hair dye	1830000	0.62
color of hair dye	1830000	0.62
color to dye hair	1830000	0.65

hair dye color	1830000	0.59
colors for hair	1830000	0.61
hair for curly hair	1500000	0.64
dye colors	1220000	0.58
colour hair dyes	1220000	0.7
dye hair colors	1220000	0.58
colors of hair dye	1220000	0.6
colors for hair dye	1220000	0.58
colors hair dye	1220000	0.56
hair colors dye	1220000	0.58
colors to dye hair	1220000	0.6
hair dye colors	1220000	0.59
color hair dyes	1220000	0.71
style short hair styles	1220000	0.36
styles with long hair	1000000	0.51
long long hair styles	1000000	0.48
hair dyes colors	823000	0.69
medium hair hairstyles	823000	0.56
medium styles	673000	0.52
medium hair hair styles	673000	0.53
hair styles with medium hair	673000	0.57
medium hair hairstyle	550000	0.51
hair for medium length hair	550000	0.57
hairstyles for face	550000	0.23
face hairstyles	550000	0.23
hairstyles face	550000	0.23
face in hairstyle	450000	0.23
face with hairstyle	450000	0.23
hairstyle for face	450000	0.23
face and hairstyle	450000	0.23
face in a hairstyle	450000	0.21
hairstyle face	450000	0.24

face hairstyle	450000	0.21
face and hair styles	450000	0.23
hair styles for face	450000	0.25
hair styles face	450000	0.24
hair styles for longhair	450000	0.57
hairstyles for faces	450000	0.28
faces and hairstyles	450000	0.27
medium hair length hairstyles	450000	0.6
medium length hair hairstyles	450000	0.56
hairstyles for long length hair	450000	0.47
hair styles for faces	450000	0.25
medium length hair styles medium length hair styles	450000	0.6
medium hair length hair styles	450000	0.62
hair styles for medium hair length	450000	0.57
hair styles medium length hair	450000	0.59
styles for guys	450000	0.85
styles guys	450000	0.84
styles with curly hair	450000	0.57
curly hair styles curly hair styles	450000	0.55
curly hair hair styles	450000	0.55
styles of curly hair	450000	0.61
hair styles curly hair	450000	0.55
hair styles for curly hair	450000	0.59
hair styles with curly hair	450000	0.57
styles curly hair	450000	0.55
style long hair styles	368000	0.45

Anthony Bissong

tips on beauty	368000	0.35
hair for a round face	368000	0.25
dye hair colours	368000	0.6
colours hair dye	368000	0.64
hair styles long length	368000	0.43
round faces hair	368000	0.26
hair round faces	368000	0.24
hairstyles for round	368000	0.26
hair round face hairstyles	368000	0.27
makeup tips makeup tips	368000	0.92
tips on makeup	368000	0.88
tips for makeup	368000	0.89
makeup tips	368000	0.94
hairstyles for round faces hairstyles for round faces	368000	0.26
hairstyles for round faces	368000	0.27

A.4 The Keywords found for the "Webindia" website using Google Keyword Tools
http://www.webindia123.com/women/tips/beauty.htm

Keyword	Global Monthly Searches	Approximate CPC (£)
makeup how to	16600000	0.62
acne	7480000	1.41
cosmetics	7480000	0.62
haircut styles	6120000	0.34
shampoo	5000000	0.55
hair color	3350000	0.6
hair colour	2740000	0.68
hair dye	2740000	0.67
waxing	2740000	0.68
home remedies	2740000	1.01
short hairstyles	2240000	0.31
hairstyles for short hair	2240000	0.32
skincare	1830000	1.16
short hair styles	1830000	0.31
day spa	1830000	1.03
mary kay	1830000	0.12
hair products	1500000	0.78
skin treatment	1220000	1.22
hairstyles for long hair	1000000	0.53
care hair	1000000	0.71
hair product	1000000	0.78
hair growth	1000000	1.44
hair treatment	1000000	1.13
hairstyles 2010	1000000	0.38
hairstyles for women	1000000	0.26
skin care treatment	1000000	1.18
hair colours	823000	0.69
hair oil	673000	0.58
makeup artist	673000	1.08

eye makeup	673000	1.01
acne treatment	673000	2.59
make up artist	673000	1.06
hair fall	550000	1.25
mens hair styles	550000	1.01
beauty parlour	550000	0.68
eye make up	550000	0.93
haircare	550000	0.67
make up artists	550000	1.01
brazilian wax	550000	0.9
how to do your hair	450000	0.93
curly hair styles	450000	0.6
beauty tips	368000	0.32
for beauty tips	368000	0.35
tips beauty	368000	0.32
tips for beauty	368000	0.31
beauty tips for	368000	0.34
tips of beauty	368000	0.33
about beauty tips	368000	0.33
tips on beauty	368000	0.35
hair treatments	368000	2.05
hair weave	368000	0.46
makeup tips	368000	0.94
tips for makeup	368000	0.89
tips on makeup	368000	0.88
how to grow hair faster	368000	0.82
make up tips	368000	0.93
tips make up	368000	0.88
bikini wax	368000	1.17
moroccan oil	368000	0.58
beauty products	301000	0.79
beauty shop	301000	0.47
hair tips	301000	0.5
tips hair	301000	0.5

tips for hair	301000	0.51
hair replacement	301000	2.84
facial care	301000	1.42
hair weaving	301000	0.44
products skin care	301000	1.42
bridal makeup	301000	0.64
skincare products	301000	1.53
wedding makeup	301000	0.67
bridal make up	301000	0.66
beautytips	301000	0.3
care beauty	246000	0.82
wedding make up	246000	0.73
best makeup	246000	1.06
make hair grow faster	246000	0.87
beauty secrets and tips	246000	0.38
beauty tips and secrets	246000	0.37
mineral makeup	201000	1.18
burts bees	201000	0.34
facial skin care	201000	1.32
facial treatment	201000	1.54
latest hairstyles	201000	0.35
how to cure pimples	201000	1.43
health and beauty	201000	0.59
vitamins for hair	201000	1.1
hair conditioner	201000	1.02
make up brushes	201000	0.78
beauty spa	201000	0.89
elle magazine	165000	0.29
hair supplies	165000	0.6
beauty makeup	165000	0.86
argan oil	165000	0.52
skin treatments	165000	1.56
healthy hair	165000	0.63
tips for girls	165000	0.52

health tips	165000	0.41
beauty tricks	165000	0.37
beauty blog	165000	0.49

A.5 The Keywords produced from using "beauty tips" in the Google Keyword Tools

Keyword	Global Monthly Searches	Approximate CPC (£)
how to be beautiful	24900000	0.48
the beauty	24900000	0.64
on beauty	24900000	0.67
about beauty	24900000	0.65
and makeup	16600000	0.65
hair styles hair	13600000	0.34
hair and styles	13600000	0.33
cosmetics	7480000	0.62
hair style	7480000	0.36
shampoo	5000000	0.55
make up cosmetics	3350000	0.45
make up and cosmetics	3350000	0.43
cosmetics and make up	3350000	0.45
beauty salon	2740000	0.75
hair loss	2240000	1.8
short hairstyles	2240000	0.31
beauty salons	2240000	0.82
skincare	1830000	1.16
short hair styles	1830000	0.31
hair styles for short hair	1830000	0.34
nail polish	1830000	0.38
mary kay	1830000	0.12
hair and beauty	1500000	0.78
beauty hair	1500000	0.77

beauty and hair	1500000	0.72
how to do make up	1500000	0.95
hair products	1500000	0.78
hairstyles 2011	1220000	0.32
beauty supply	1220000	0.22
hairstyles for long hair	1000000	0.53
hair care	1000000	0.75
how to care for hair	1000000	0.69
care hair	1000000	0.71
hair growth	1000000	1.44
hair treatment	1000000	1.13
beauty supplies	1000000	0.22
bridal hair	823000	0.39
face mask	823000	0.62
nail and beauty	673000	1.11
beauty and nail	673000	1.14
makeup artist	673000	1.08
eye makeup	673000	1.01
make up artist	673000	1.06
beauty parlor	550000	0.72
hair fall	550000	1.25
beauty parlour	550000	0.68
eye make up	550000	0.93
make up for eyes	550000	1.13
haircare	550000	0.67
make up artists	550000	1.01
beauty treatments	450000	0.94
facial mask	450000	0.61
how to braid hair	450000	0.36
about beauty tips	368000	0.33
beauty tips for	368000	0.34
tips for beauty	368000	0.31
tips of beauty	368000	0.33
tips beauty	368000	0.32

how to beauty tips	368000	0.32
for beauty tips	368000	0.35
beauty tips from	368000	0.35
tips to beauty	368000	0.32
tips on beauty	368000	0.35
tips about beauty	368000	0.33
wedding hair styles	368000	0.29
makeup tips	368000	0.94
tips for makeup	368000	0.89
tips on makeup	368000	0.88
tips makeup	368000	0.9
how to grow hair faster	368000	0.82
make up tips	368000	0.93
tips make up	368000	0.88
tips for make up	368000	0.87
make up tips for	368000	0.88
tips on make up	368000	0.85
tips of make up	368000	0.94
hair ideas	368000	0.56
beauty products	301000	0.79
in beauty products	301000	0.79
face care	301000	1.15
beautician	301000	2.66
care for women	301000	1.97
beauty shop	301000	0.47
hair tips	301000	0.5
tips for hair	301000	0.51
tips hair	301000	0.5
tips on hair	301000	0.49
makeup forever	301000	0.21
hair and makeup	301000	0.66
skin care products	301000	1.42
hair regrowth	301000	1.66
how to do makeup	301000	1.1

bridal makeup	301000	0.64
free make up	301000	0.68
make up free	301000	0.72
make up for free	301000	0.74
make up online	301000	0.84
wedding makeup	301000	0.67
bridal make up	301000	0.66
beautytips	301000	0.3
beauty care	246000	0.81
beauty and care	246000	0.77
care beauty	246000	0.82
beauty & care	246000	0.85
wedding make up	246000	0.73
best make up	246000	1.04
best makeup	246000	1.06
hair up styles	246000	0.31
natural beauty	246000	0.39
beauty natural	246000	0.41
beauty tips and secrets	246000	0.37
beauty secrets and tips	246000	0.38
beauty secrets tips	246000	0.35
beauty tips secrets	246000	0.37
beauty therapy	201000	0.88
mineral makeup	201000	1.18
make up hair	201000	0.68
health and beauty	201000	0.59
skin for men	201000	0.93
online beauty	201000	1.18
hair conditioner	201000	1.02
mask hair	201000	0.44
make up brushes	201000	0.78
face make up	201000	0.51
make up face	201000	0.5
make up for face	201000	0.5

Anthony Bissong

virtual makeover	201000	0.37
care for men	201000	1.56
beauty video	165000	0.55
free beauty	165000	0.64
beauty makeup	165000	0.86
makeup and beauty	165000	0.88
beauty and makeup	165000	0.82
makeup beauty	165000	0.78
skin and beauty	165000	0.93
beauty and skin	165000	0.96
skin & beauty	165000	0.93
threading eyebrows	165000	0.71
healthy hair	165000	0.63
tips for girls	165000	0.52
health tips	165000	0.41
tips for health	165000	0.4
tips health	165000	0.45
tips on health	165000	0.4
beauty tricks	165000	0.37
fashion secrets	165000	0.49
beauty blog	165000	0.49
beauty cosmetics	165000	0.73
beauty tips and tricks	165000	0.35
beauty tips tricks	165000	0.35
beauty tricks and tips	165000	0.39
beauty tricks and secrets	165000	0.39
beauty tricks secrets	165000	0.39
how to apply makeup	135000	1.03
how to apply make up	135000	1.13
anti aging cream	135000	1.39
how to grow long hair	135000	0.85
on line beauty	135000	1.08
facial products	135000	1.21
skin tips	135000	0.61

tips for skin	135000	0.55
tips skin	135000	0.54
hair spa	135000	0.7
face skin care	135000	1.22
skin care face	135000	1.21
make up beauty	135000	0.82
beauty make up	135000	0.78
make up and beauty	135000	0.76
beauty and make up	135000	0.76
skin makeup	135000	1.07
makeup for skin	135000	1.15
celebrities makeup	135000	0.59
best hair products	135000	1.27
make up blog	110000	0.47
make up skin	110000	1.02
skin make up	110000	1.06
make up for skin	110000	1.13
mineral foundation	110000	0.93
nails and beauty	110000	1.18
beauty and nails	110000	1.21
makeup face	110000	0.86
hair care products	110000	0.89
nail care	110000	0.67
nails care	110000	0.53
celebrity makeup	110000	0.63
how to put on makeup	110000	1.06
how to put makeup on	110000	1.02
celebrity make up	110000	0.61
make up celebrity	110000	0.68
face tips	110000	0.25
tips for face	110000	0.26
tips face	110000	0.25
how to get long hair	110000	0.79
make up ideas	110000	1.08

makeup ideas	90500	1.05
make up tutorials	90500	1.19
best mascara	90500	0.96
natural make up	90500	1.17
eyebrow shaping	90500	0.79
make up tricks	90500	0.82
makeup blog	90500	0.67
makeup tricks	90500	0.81
tips for fashion	90500	0.48
fashion tips and	90500	0.44
glowing skin	90500	0.44
natural makeup	90500	1.18
cosmetics online	90500	0.55
cheap makeup	90500	0.65
hair care product	90500	0.87
make up tips and tricks	90500	0.8
make up tricks and tips	90500	0.74
makeup tips and ideas	90500	1.05
makeup tips and tricks	90500	0.79
makeup tricks and tips	90500	0.74
makeup tips tricks	90500	0.81
makeup looks	90500	1.08
short curly hairstyles	90500	0.45
style tips	90500	0.43
natural hair care	90500	1.12
hair care natural	90500	1.09
short black hair styles	90500	0.28
natural skin care	90500	1.78
skin care natural	90500	1.67
food for hair	90500	0.78
make up looks	90500	1.1
how to prevent hair loss	74000	1.38
best eye cream	74000	1.14
make up samples	74000	0.66

samples make up	74000	0.64
short curly hair styles	74000	0.45
how to apply eyeliner	74000	0.99
make up men	74000	0.68
make up for men	74000	0.75
men make up	74000	0.71
men and make up	74000	0.74
make up for man	74000	0.5
hair growth products	74000	1.99
tips for eyes	74000	1.2
make up alley	74000	0.96
beauty forums	74000	0.29
makeup for men	74000	0.69
men and makeup	74000	0.7
hair growth oil	74000	0.86
black hair products	60500	1.05
beauty for men	60500	0.69
black hair care	60500	0.99
mary kay cosmetics	60500	0.17
make up for women	60500	0.99
women make up	60500	0.98
women and make up	60500	0.91
makeup for women	60500	0.97
how to apply eyeshadow	60500	1.11
beauty magazine	60500	0.32
make up products	60500	0.8
makeup products	60500	0.75
hair styles tips	60500	0.36
tips for hair styles	60500	0.39
hair tips and styles	60500	0.36
hair styles and tips	60500	0.34
tips on hair styles	60500	0.34
website beauty	60500	1.35
free makeup samples	49500	0.61

beauty skin care	49500	1.02
skin care beauty	49500	1.1
beauty care skin	49500	1.12
beauty and skin care	49500	1.09
skin care and beauty	49500	1.04
secret beauty tips	49500	0.64
beauty quiz	49500	0.19
free make up samples	49500	0.62
skin care for men	49500	1.85
men skin care	49500	1.89
skin care men	49500	1.95
for men skin care	49500	1.92
men and skin care	49500	1.82
free make up sample	49500	0.6
hair health	49500	1.33
health hair	49500	1.34
bridal tips	49500	0.62
make up body	49500	0.67
make up for body	49500	0.63
simple make up	49500	1
hair tips and tricks	49500	0.55
hair tricks and tips	49500	0.52
discount make up	40500	0.61
make up styles	40500	0.87
styles make up	40500	0.92
free cosmetic samples	40500	0.64
organic make up	40500	1.21
free cosmetics	40500	0.76
eye make up tips	40500	1.04
make up videos	40500	0.8
fashion make up	40500	0.63
makeup application	40500	1.2
discount cosmetics	40500	0.55
skin care tips	40500	0.75

tips for skin care	40500	0.79
tips skin care	40500	0.75
tips on skin care	40500	0.76
tips to skin care	40500	0.73
makeup styles	33100	0.99
free make up online	33100	0.72
beauty recipes	33100	0.29
beauty flash	33100	0.39
beauty blogs	33100	0.53
beauty in urdu	33100	0.15
urdu beauty	33100	0.14
prom make up	33100	1.03
very short hairstyles	33100	0.29
organic makeup	33100	1.12
beauty tips in urdu	33100	0.14
urdu beauty tips	33100	0.14
beauty tips urdu	33100	0.14
makeup for me	33100	0.72
bridal makeup artist	33100	0.68
beauty news	33100	0.53
female make up	33100	0.94
how to apply eye makeup	33100	1.06
very short hair styles	27100	0.31
organic cosmetics	27100	1.01
mineral cosmetics	27100	1.21
free make up cosmetics	27100	0.68
wedding makeup artist	27100	0.67
skin beauty products	27100	1.08
get free make up	27100	0.56
usa make up	27100	0.53
eye makeup for brown eyes	27100	1.41
skin care beauty	27100	1.13

products		
beauty and skin care products	27100	1.02
hair skin care	27100	0.67
hair and skin care	27100	0.7
skin and hair care	27100	0.67
skin care hair	27100	0.74
skin care hair care	27100	0.67
skin care and hair care	27100	0.72
hair care skin care	27100	0.72
tips for glowing skin	22200	0.25
beauty tips for face	22200	0.14
face beauty tips	22200	0.14
beauty tips face	22200	0.14
beauty tips of face	22200	0.13
beauty tips for the face	22200	0.14
beauty tips on face	22200	0.15
beauty tips in face	22200	0.15
beauty face tips	22200	0.15
tips for beauty face	22200	0.13
tips for face beauty	22200	0.14
skin care beauty product	22200	1.11
home beauty tips	22200	0.23
beauty tips at home	22200	0.25
beauty tips in home	22200	0.22
at home beauty tips	22200	0.24
beauty home tips	22200	0.24
home tips for beauty	22200	0.24
applying makeup	22200	1.06
make up care	22200	0.76
indian bridal makeup	22200	0.45
free beauty samples	22200	0.7
facial tips	22200	0.82

80 make up	22200	0.31
hair care tips	22200	0.58
tips for hair care	22200	0.57
tips on hair care	22200	0.61
tips hair care	22200	0.58
hair facts	22200	1.11
make up eyebrows	22200	1
make up for eyebrows	22200	0.97
beauty products face	22200	1.13
face beauty products	22200	1.06
mens skin care	22200	1.94
hair growth tips	22200	0.52
tips for hair growth	22200	0.51
homemade beauty tips	22200	0.22
beauty tips homemade	22200	0.21
beauty homemade tips	22200	0.22
makeup for guys	18100	0.61
beauty bible	18100	0.29
make up secrets	18100	0.35
hair fall control	18100	0.35
how to control hair fall	18100	0.38
80 makeup	18100	0.36
make up blogs	18100	0.56
loreal hair products	18100	0.46
beautiful tips	18100	0.42
how to be beautiful tips	18100	0.39
tips to be beautiful	18100	0.41
tips for healthy hair	18100	0.27
healthy hair tips	18100	0.27
hairstyle tips	18100	0.55
tips for hair style	18100	0.73
hair style tips	18100	0.71
free beauty sample	18100	0.64
teen make up	18100	0.77

long hair tips	18100	0.5
skin care for women	18100	1.91
skin care women	18100	1.82
home made beauty tips	18100	0.2
beauty tip	18100	0.42
tip of beauty	18100	0.44
homemade beauty recipes	14800	0.21
information on make up	14800	0.63
hair styling tips	14800	0.66
hair care for men	14800	1.8
make up for lips	14800	0.73
beauty advice	14800	0.67
makeup lips	14800	0.85
hair beauty products	14800	0.65
beauty products hair	14800	0.58
natural beauty tips	14800	0.31
beauty tips natural	14800	0.3
natural tips for beauty	14800	0.29
beauty natural tips	14800	0.27
tips for natural beauty	14800	0.28
make up and hairstyles	14800	0.46
beauty tips for skin	14800	0.31
skin beauty tips	14800	0.33
beauty tips skin	14800	0.34
beauty tips for the skin	14800	0.33
beauty skin tips	14800	0.34
skin and beauty tips	14800	0.32
beauty tips of skin	14800	0.31
tips for beauty skin	14800	0.33
skin care cosmetics	14800	1.04
makeup and beauty blog	14800	0.41

makeup beauty products	14800	0.77
beauty products makeup	14800	0.82
hair products online	12100	0.55
make beauty products	12100	0.78
make up techniques	12100	1.05
eyeshadow tips	12100	1.24
makeup tips for brown eyes	12100	1.36
skin care free	12100	1.25
natural beauty products	12100	1.26
beauty products natural	12100	1.29
beauty tips for girls	12100	0.46
girls beauty tips	12100	0.48
beauty tips girls	12100	0.48
fashion hair for men	12100	0.46
beauty articles	12100	0.59
articles beauty	12100	0.59
eyeliner tips	12100	0.99
tips for hairstyles	12100	0.59
home beauty secrets	12100	0.27
mira hair oil	12100	0.27
nail service	12100	0.67
facial beauty treatments	12100	1.32
hair tips for men	12100	1.4
hair tips men	12100	1.33
mary kay products	12100	0.28
hair care for women	12100	1.6
women hair care	12100	1.49
make up and hair styles	12100	0.54
hair and make up	12100	0.53

styles		
make up hair styles	12100	0.51
tips for lips	12100	0.59
homemade beauty secrets	12100	0.25
make skin care	12100	1.1
make up ideas for eyes	12100	1.31
natural beauty care	12100	1.16
make up info	9900	0.48
beauty products make up	9900	0.76
make up and beauty products	9900	0.84
beauty products online	9900	0.82
online beauty products	9900	0.82
home tips for hair	9900	0.44
beauty styles	9900	1.34
beauty advisor	9900	0.52
natural beauty secrets	9900	0.27
make up your face	9900	0.95
make up nail	9900	0.59
hair care beauty	9900	0.79
hair care and beauty	9900	0.84
bridal makeup tips	9900	0.58
beauty tips for hair	9900	0.27
hair beauty tips	9900	0.25
beauty tips hair	9900	0.26
hair and beauty tips	9900	0.27
beauty hair tips	9900	0.26
beauty and hair tips	9900	0.24
beauty tips of hair	9900	0.27
beauty tips about hair	9900	0.25
beauty tips on hair	9900	0.27
on line beauty products	9900	0.94

beauty hair style	9900	2.09
hair style beauty	9900	2.06
bridal make up tips	9900	0.61
wedding makeup tips	9900	0.59
bridal makeup pictures	9900	0.48
fairness tips	8100	0.1
beauty tips in hindi	8100	0.16
hindi beauty tips	8100	0.15
beauty tips hindi	8100	0.16
hair tips in urdu	8100	0.18
urdu hair tips	8100	0.19
urdu tips for hair	8100	0.18
hair tips urdu	8100	0.19
hair beauty product	8100	0.55
eye makeup tricks	8100	0.85
health beauty products	8100	0.91
eye make up tricks	8100	0.85
home tips for skin	8100	0.31
make up health	8100	0.62
best beauty tips	8100	0.51
the best beauty tips	8100	0.56
beauty tips for women	8100	0.73
women beauty tips	8100	0.78
beauty tips women	8100	0.74
make up advice	8100	0.98
makeup advice	8100	0.95
make up nails	6600	0.6
make up and nails	6600	0.59
nails make up	6600	0.54
beauty skin treatment	6600	0.99
natural tips for hair	6600	0.46
free beauty products	6600	1.09
beauty product reviews	6600	0.73

free beauty cosmetics	6600	0.7
urdu tips for skin	6600	0.15
skin tips urdu	6600	0.15
skin tips in urdu	6600	0.14
urdu skin tips	6600	0.14
beauty hair styles	6600	1.39
hair makeup styles	6600	0.54
hair and makeup styles	6600	0.56
beauty tips and advice	6600	0.54
beauty advice and tips	6600	0.52
skin care makeup	6600	1.26
skin care and makeup	6600	1.25
makeup skin care	6600	1.26
makeup and skin care	6600	1.27
hair and makeup tips	6600	1.05
makeup and hair tips	6600	1.15
hair makeup tips	6600	1.17
makeover tips	6600	0.95
hair tips for women	6600	0.77
makeup help	6600	1.25
makeup in urdu	6600	0.29
hair and make up tips	6600	1.08
make up and hair tips	6600	1.07
skin care make up	5400	1.12
make up skin care	5400	1.1
make up and skin care	5400	1.23
skin care and make up	5400	1.24
face cover up	5400	0.69
beauty tips in tamil	5400	0.11
tamil beauty tips	5400	0.11
beauty tips tamil	5400	0.11
beauty tips for tamil	5400	0.12
beauty tips for men	5400	0.35
men beauty tips	5400	0.31

beauty tips men	5400	0.33
style tips for men	5400	0.89
beauty products samples	5400	1.12
samples beauty products	5400	1.06
natural eye make up	5400	1.44
eye make up natural	5400	1.33
skin care secrets	5400	0.75
health care tips	5400	1.08
beautiful products	5400	0.86
skin care for man	5400	1.42
skin care secret	5400	0.72
health tips in urdu	5400	0.28
urdu health tips	5400	0.26
urdu tips for health	5400	0.27
health tips urdu	5400	0.27

A.6 Beauty Tips Top Ranked Blogs Found

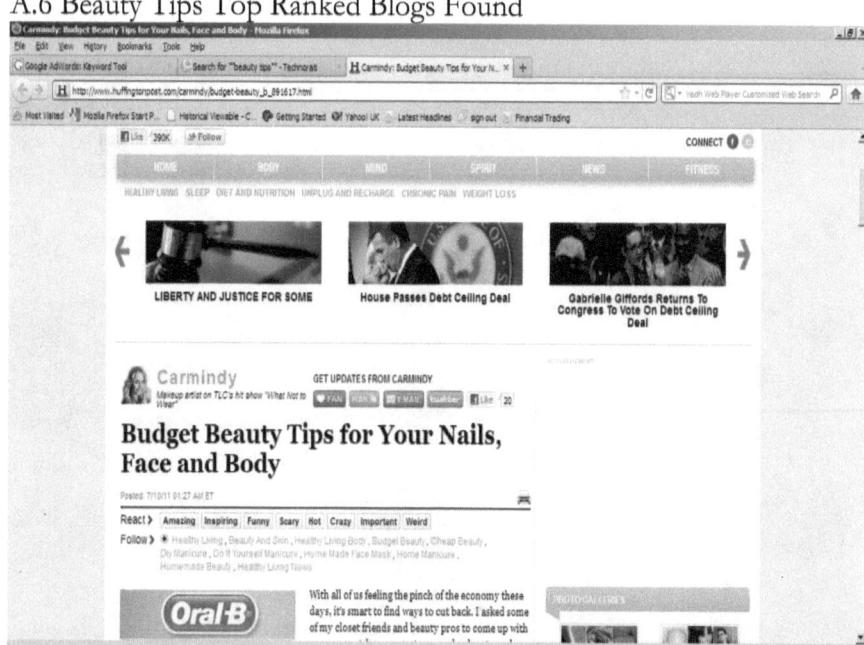

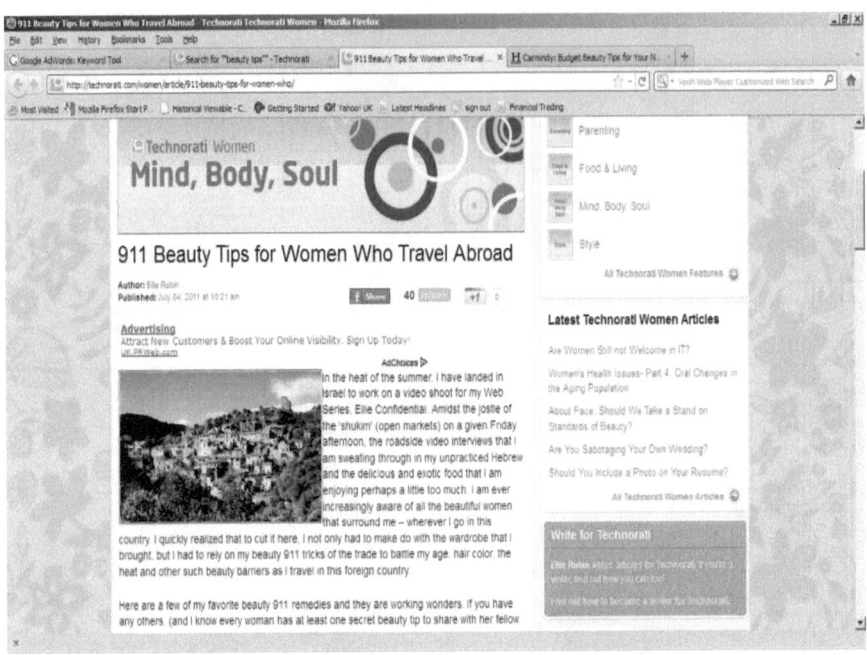

A Simple Guide For Starting A Legitimate Home Business Online

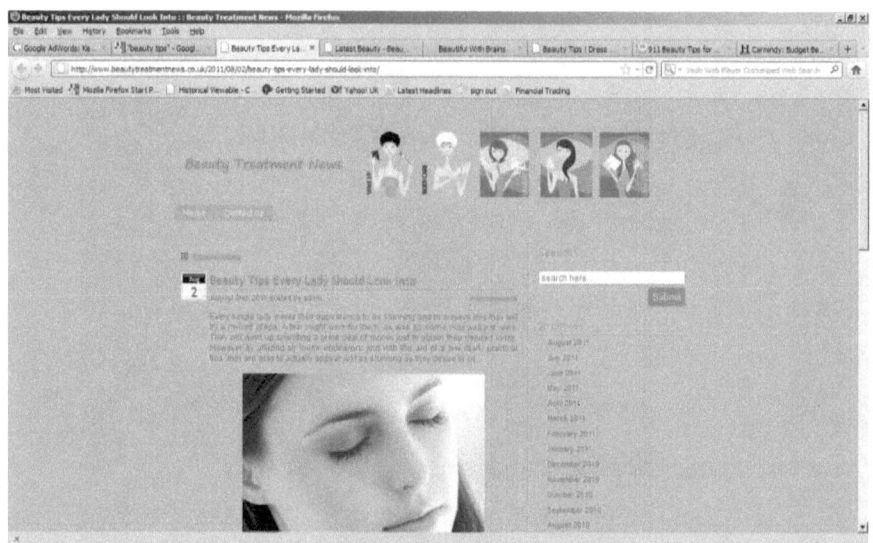

A.7 Beauty Tips Forums

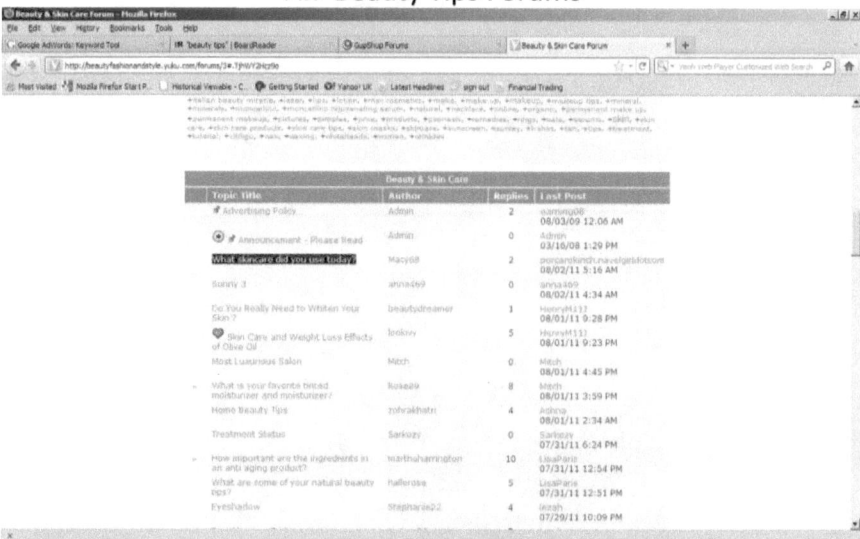

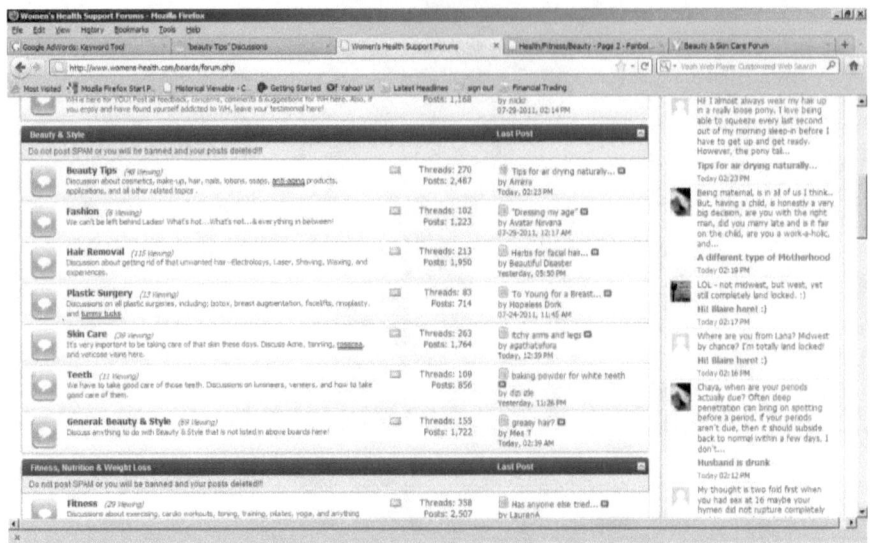

END